Money
and Inflation

Money
and Inflation

FRANK HAHN

The MIT Press
Cambridge, Massachusetts

First MIT Press edition, 1983

© Frank Hahn 1981

First published 1981
Basil Blackwell Publisher, England

Library of Congress catalog card number 82-61259
ISBN 0-262-08129-6

Printed and bound in the United States of America

Contents

Foreword

The publication of Professor Hahn's lectures marks the beginning of a new venture. Hitherto the Mitsui Lectures in Economics have consisted of only one lecture given annually. From now on three lectures will be delivered, permitting the lecturer more scope to develop his material; and to allow adequate time for preparation, the lectures will be held biennially. In addition they will be made available to a wider audience by their publication in book form.

This change in format would not have been possible without the generous financial assistance that has been received from Mitsui & Co. Ltd. Indeed, that assistance has been of such magnitude that it has been possible for us to make the Mitsui Lectures an international series. So far we have only planned ahead to 1983; the lectures will then be given by Professor James Tobin.

Mitsui & Co. Ltd has had strong connections with the Faculty of Commerce and Social Science and with the Department of Economics at the University of Birmingham since shortly after the granting of the University charter in 1900. Members of the Mitsui family and junior members of the firm singled out for promotion came to the University to study as occasional students. In 1923 Baron Hachiroyemon Mitsui donated a substantial amount of money to the University for the establishment of a Chair of Finance; in 1946 the title was changed to the Chair of Economics. The Mitsui company has maintained its interest in the University and has continued to support students in various fields of study. In recent years it has financed research into Anglo-Japanese trade as well as the Mitsui Lectures. We are indeed grateful for all the support and encouragement we have received from the company.

The theme of the Mitsui Lectures can be theoretical, empirical or both; the only brief given to the lecturers is that the topic should be a major one within economics. In that way we hope that the series will make a significant contribution to the literature, either by offering a critical review of the current situation, or by providing new insights into the way forward, or by combining the two.

We have been especially fortunate in persuading Professor Frank Hahn to launch the new series. For there can be no doubt that he has selected a topic of paramount importance for theory and policy and (as would be expected) he has made a major contribution to the established literature in both areas, despite his own reservations and modesty. It would be inappropriate of me to preempt what he has to say on money and inflation, but I can perhaps be permitted to echo one of the obviously heartfelt sentiments expressed in his Preface. It is at once irritating and worrying to witness so much faith being placed by governments in their policy-making in the (rational expectations) Monetarist models of money, output and inflation; models that are simplistic from a theoretical view and for which, especially for their central message that money is neutral, there is no adequate empirical support.

J. L. Ford

Preface

I was much flattered when the Birmingham University economists invited me to deliver the Mitsui Lectures for 1981 and I thank them for doing so. The result, which is to be found in the following pages, is highly imperfect. This can be ascribed to a number of causes, apart from my own shortcomings.

In many places, my arguments lack the rigorous support that only formal modelling can provide. This is due only partly to the constraints imposed by public lectures to a varied audience. Much more important has been my view that much that is of central significance to my theme, cannot be understood in the framework of Walrasian equilibrium. This has meant that many of the tools and concepts that constitute much of my intellectual capital were not available. To argue with the rigour of general equilibrium theory when studying what seems to be essential characteristics of labour markets, and to weave these into a precise model of the whole economy, is, at the moment, beyond me. I have therefore on occasions had to rest satisfied with arguments that are merely plausible rather than clinching. I am naturally fairly confident that they will in due course be clinched, but I am aware that they have not always been so far.

Partly for these reasons, I have given a good deal of attention to the more familiar models, and especially to those that invoke rational expectations. I am concerned to argue that some of the claims now current for monetary economies of this kind are not logically entailed. In this, I have probably devoted too much attention to the economists whom I label 'Lucasians' – not that the best of them are not worthy of attention, but the reader may perhaps find too much that is purely critical or technical. On the other hand, I do regard this criticism as of some importance at a time when many in power seem to have been persuaded that 'economic science' supports what one may loosely call Monetarist policies.

Indeed, in places I find that I am not only polemical but perhaps close to being strident. This is in part to be explained, and I hope excused, by the current state of affairs in Britain. To witness the unfolding of policies that, it is claimed, have the support of the best economic theory, when one knows this to be false, is quite a trial. When one then finds that one cannot read a newspaper without coming across some economists expounding the opening chapters of an elementary theory textbook as if it had descriptive certainty, one is stretched very far. And when one turns to the best of the new orthodox and finds that they exclude the possibility of someone willing to work at the current wage but not finding a job, by assumption and not by argument, then a little stridency may be just what is needed.

It is of course true that the Keynesian orthodoxy was also flimsily based and that its practitioners also dealt in unwarranted certainties: I do not wish to defend this. But bygones are bygones, and these economists are not now stridently to the forefront. However, I ought to lay my cards on the table. I consider that Keynes had no real grasp of formal economic theorizing (and also disliked it), and that he consequently left many gaping holes in his theory. I none the less hold that his insights were several orders more profound and realistic than those of his recent critics. These insights seem to me to make it impossible to take a Walrasian long-run equilibrium, or for that matter a rational expectations equilibrium, as descriptively satisfactory. I still regard these constructions as useful scaffolding, but no more. Accordingly, in these lectures I follow various Keynesian trails in an endeavour to reach a point where theory is not so blatantly at variance with fact.

On the other hand, a good deal that occupies me has been the staple of monetary theory for a long time. Why do agents hold money? Is money neutral? Superneutral? Is an expanding money supply a necessary condition for inflation? And so on. I think that, even so, some of the things I have to say may be new. But of course a great many things have been said by others before. I have given references where I knew them, but the literature is so large that I am sure that I have missed a good many. The intention has not been to deprive anyone of credit or precedence, but to have done.

I have been fortunate in persuading some of my friends to read these lectures as they were first delivered, and to send me comments. Robert Solow, Kenneth Arrow, Oliver Hart, Mark Machina, Douglas Gale and Eric Maskin all did this, and in the process saved me from both some silliness and some mistakes. Eric Maskin persuaded me that my original analysis of what I call the natural rate of inflation was at fault, Mark Machina and Douglas Gale extended my result on rational expectations equilibria with money and bonds. Douglas Gale provided detailed comments on lectures I and II and made me rethink the question of the determinateness of the price level. On some other matters, however, we did not reach agreement. In any case, owing to their efforts, the lectures are not the same as when they were first delivered. I am grateful to all of them and also to Clare Blenkinsop for typing the lectures, and to Richard Pitbladdo for proofreading and indexing.

There is one last point. I often refer to 'Monetarists'. In many ways, such a blanket term is undesirable, especially if one is not friendly. I have myself often objected to the use of 'Neoclassical' on similar occasions; but I don't know what to do about it, short of referring each time to named papers, which I didn't think appropriate here. In any case, I must warn the reader that there may be those who call themselves Monetarists but repudiate some of the views I ascribe to this group.

F.H.H.
June 1981

I

Foundations

The most serious challenge that the existence of money poses to the theorist is this: the best developed model of the economy cannot find room for it. The best developed model is, of course, the Arrow–Debreu version of a Walrasian general equilibrium. A world in which all conceivable contingent future contracts are possible neither needs nor wants intrinsically worthless money. A first, and to a fastidious theorist difficult, task is to find an alternative construction without thereby sacrificing the clarity and logical coherence that are such outstanding features of Arrow–Debreu.

The point is obvious and has been made quite often. But it is doubtful that it has been fully taken on board. Here is an example. Friedman (1969) argued that a positive shadow price of money balances would violate the Pareto-efficiency condition that the shadow price of anything should equal its marginal cost. For the latter can be taken as zero in the case of paper money. From this, he then deduced that the optimum quantity of money is larger than that which prevails in economies in which money is held and has a positive opportunity cost. Others have advocated paying interest on money holdings. But if it is the case that a monetary economy is not an Arrow–Debreu economy, then classical welfare theorems applicable in the latter may not survive in the former. For instance, the lack of markets may mean that private agents are constrained by many budget constraints, so that the Pareto efficiency of any equilibrium must be in doubt. Or if, in this non-Arrow–Debreu world, the holding of money is to provide the insurance that would otherwise have been provided by contingent futures markets, and if satiation in money balances demanded by Friedman requires 'full' insurance, then, as Bewley (1980) has shown, no finite money stock may accomplish that. So one is certainly in danger of making mistakes if one simply applies results from Arrow–Debreu analysis to a monetary economy.

In any case it is now agreed, and it is becoming widely understood, that a minimal requirement for a theory of a monetary economy is that the latter should have trading at every date. Radner (1968) has christened such economies *sequence economies*. Such sequences are required if it is to be rational to hold money at any date; any agent voluntarily holding money balances that have a positive exchange value must do so on the understanding that they can be exchanged at some future date. Putting money into the utility function, while harmless if properly done and interpreted, can also and has also held back the development of a proper monetary theory. It certainly cannot save us from having to consider sequence economies.

The step to sequence economies[1] has quite decisive consequences for economic theory; for if there are transactions at every date, then the agent must also, in making his plans at any date, form expectations about market conditions at future dates. In an Arrow–Debreu economy, expectations enter only in so far as they reflect beliefs

---

[1] The step was first taken by the Swedes (e.g. Lundberg, 1937; Myrdal, 1939); and by Hicks (1939).

concerning states of nature. Will it be wet or fine tomorrow? Such expectations continue to be required in a sequence economy, but they must now be supplemented by market expectations: what will prices be tomorrow if fine, what if wet? Since we need a sequence picture as a necessary prerequisite for monetary theory, it now follows that there is no way of avoiding the issue of market expectations either.

One of Keynes's claims to the title of great economist is that he saw this more clearly than any of his predecessors had done – and, indeed, more clearly than many of his successors. One of the dangers, for instance, of the *IS–LM* tradition is that it leads easily to a neglect of expectational variables, and scores of textbooks testify to the confusion that results. In any case: no monetary theory without sequences, and no sequences without expectations.

But now we are in trouble. We have no theory of expectations firmly founded on elementary principles comparable say, to our theory of consumer choice. Clearly, expectations must be based on the agent's observations, which of course is meant to include the history of such observations. But as I have noted elsewhere (Hahn, 1973b), the transformation of observation into expectations requires the agent to hold a theory, or, if you like, requires him to have a model. This model itself will not be independent of the history of observations. Indeed, learning largely consists of updating of models of this kind. Although we have Bayes's theorem, very little is known about such learning in an economic context. There is thus a great temptation to short-circuit the problem, at least in a first approach, and to consider only economic states in which learning has ceased. These will be states in which the realization of expected variables provides no disconfirmation of the theory and the beliefs held in the light of that theory and the past realization of the variables. Thus, in such states, the probability distribution over economic

3

variables that agents hold cause them to take actions which in turn generate just this probability distribution. This is the idea of a *rational expectations equilibrium*.

In the course of these lectures, I shall have a good deal to say about such equilibria. At this stage, I only want to draw attention to one point. We avoid the trouble caused by our ignorance of expectation formation by asking a question in the answer to which the precise manner in which expectations are formed plays no role. Roughly, the question is: what must expectations be if actions based on these expectations are to lead to outcomes that confirm the expectations? What lends interest to this question is a very general and plausible axiom of expectation formation: expectations that are systematically falsified will be changed. So one is, in some sense, looking for stable or maintainable expectations. But as in all equilibrium analysis, one cannot proceed from this hypothetical construct to the world either without a theory of how it comes about or by an act of faith. Many economists, as I will later document, have opted for the latter. Others have realized that they need mistakes in expectations or insufficient information to explain commonplace occurrences, such as fluctuations in output and employment. If these mistakes are of the kind that allow agents to learn from them, then an expectation formation hypothesis is required. The trouble caused by our lack of adequate theory of expectation formation (or for that matter price formation) is avoided only by a very considerable narrowing of the questions that we ask. The dangers of this will, I hope, become clear as I proceed.

But let me now return to the main line of the argument. We have agreed that a theory of a monetary economy requires us to think of a sequence of markets, and that this entails explicit attention to market expectations. Suppose that, in the first instance, we think of such a sequence economy in rational expectations equilibrium. A problem arises if we model such an economy as being of finite duration. If there is a last date, then clearly at that date no agent will wish to hold paper money – it must be worthless. But this, under rational expectations, is known to agents at the moment preceding the final date. If they hold money to transfer to the final date, they will be forgoing current consumption for no future benefit. So no one will wish to hold paper money at the moment preceding the final date, and it will thus also be worthless at that moment. Proceeding in this way, and always invoking rational expectations, we easily deduce that money must be worthless at every date, and so we will have failed in constructing a theory of a monetary economy. From this, we conclude that we cannot have a rational expectations monetary theory in an economy lasting a finite length of time unless we introduce a new and largely *ad hoc* element into the story. This might take the form of postulating that there is an inescapable law requiring agents to pay fixed money sums to the government at the final date. This is the route that I and others chose (Hahn, 1971) as a device to avoid infinities, but it is not particularly satisfactory.

The conclusion that we need infinitely long-lived economies in order to model money in rational expectations equilibrium has been taken very seriously by some economists (e.g. Cass and Shell, 1980). This is rather unfortunate, since, as I understand it, the laws of physics provide an absolutely certain upper bound on the life of the solar system. We have here a case where a convenient abstraction – rational expectations – is being driven without sensitivity to an uninteresting and, in the final analysis, absurd conclusion.

What we really need, as Grandmont and Younes (1972) have noted, is that, at every date we are interested in, each agent should attach positive probability to money having a positive exchange value at the next date. We are interested in states in which this belief is not falsified at almost any of the dates that we consider. We allow, if we are thinking of a finite horizon, say 10,000 years from now, the penultimate man or woman to be mistaken; for we know that this departure from rational expectations is quite unimportant, and that we are capturing all that we want to capture: a positive exchange value of money for long periods based on beliefs that, again for long periods, are not falsified.

While one cannot, then, take seriously the view that finitely lived economies would have no money, this of course does not mean that, as theorists, we should not work with infinite time horizons. This quite often is the most convenient procedure. My argument is simply that we should avoid a leaden literalness when we employ such devices.

Suppose, then, that we consider an infinitely long-lived economy in rational expectations equilibrium. Can we now be sure that money has a positive exchange value in such an equilibrium? To answer that question, we need to consider the more particular structure of the model to which this question is addressed. Before I do that I should like to insert an explanatory remark to those who do not habitually engage in this kind of economic theory. In looking for conditions that will suffice to ensure a positive exchange value for money at every date, we are looking into two kinds of related problems. First, what are the properties and functions of money? Second, what features of an economy do we need to model in order that there is indeed room for money to perform its functions to render it valuable at any date? The questions may appear abstract – indeed, wilfully so. After all, none of us, in spite of the efforts of government and oil sheikhs, has ever experienced a valueless pound. But anyone who has ever thought about a paper money economy has concluded that this is a circumstance that needs a good deal of explaining. Until we have done so, no satisfactory answers to more practical monetary questions are likely.

In recent years, a good many models have been constructed in which money serves only as a store of value. We already know that this is a necessary function for money if it is to perform any function at all. The question is whether it is sufficient. It will not be hard to show that it is not. By this, I mean that, if we regard money purely as a device for accomplishing an intertemporal reallocation of consumption, then one can generally exhibit rational expectations equilibria where this device does not work because money is valueless. This can be done quite generally (Hahn, 1965) but at this point it may be useful to be more specific.

Let us consider the fashionable model of overlapping generations first used to brilliant effect by Samuelson (1958). Since I shall use this model again later for other purposes, it will be useful to be precise, although all the main lessons can be learned by keeping it simple.

We are to imagine a world where agents live for two periods. At any time, then, the economy consists of the young and the old. For the moment, it will suffice if we look at a situation of pure exchange. That is, we will see to it that the young and old are provided with exogenous endowment. In particular, if there is a single good and money, we assume that there is an endowment of the good available to each person at the beginning of each period of his life. When the story starts, the old have all the money there is. Realizing their imminent demise, they will want to convert it into consumption. This they can do only by inducing the young to accept money in exchange for the good. Nothing is lost by assuming there to be one person of each age. It is trivial to extend the analysis to a growing population.

Measuring all prices in terms of money, we can write the budget constraints of the young at the beginning of their lives as follows:

$$p_t c_t^y + m_t^y \leqslant p_t e_t^y$$

$$p_{t+1}^e c_{t+1}^y \leqslant p_{t+1}^e e_{t+1}^y + m_t^y.$$

Here c_t^y is the consumption of the young at t; m_t^y is their demand for money balances; e_t^y is their endowment at t, and p_{t+1}^e is the money price of the good expected by them at t to rule at date $(t + 1)$. We make two observations. (1) I am here taking the simplest case of single valued expectations. This will be dropped presently. (2) I shall be assuming that the money stock in the economy is constant. This too, will be dropped later.

As usual, we endow the young with well-behaved preferences over consumption at the two dates. As usual also, they make a consumption plan, and so, implicitly, a plan for holding money, such that no other plan satisfying the budget constraints is preferred to it. Then, taking endowments as given, we may write the consumption demand[2] of the young at date t as

$$c_t^y = \gamma^y(p_t, p_{t+1}^e).$$

It is immediate that this function is homogeneous of degree zero in the two money prices. So if we write $q_t^e = (p_{t+1}^e)/(p_t)$, we may also write (without change in functional notation)

$$c_t^y = \gamma^y(q_t^e).$$

---

[2] I assume strictly convex preferences so that the preference-optimizing choice is unique.

For future reference we now make the following further observation. The number q_t^e represents the terms at which the young believe that they can transform present into future consumption. Consider the consumption plan (c_t^y, c_{t+1}^y), which results in the young not trading with the old at all. Through this point, there passes an indifference curve (which I assume differentiable) with a slope of $\bar{q}$. The interpretation is that, if the terms of trade between present and future consumption were $\bar{q}$, the young would do best for themselves by not trading at all. Since there is no borrowing possible, we must have $c_t^y \leqslant e_t^y$. But when $q_t^e > \bar{q}$, the young would wish to borrow if they could, a proposition that can be checked by an elementary application of the axiom of revealed preference. Hence, for all $q_t^e \geqslant \bar{q}$, the young will not wish to trade; or, put differently, a necessary, and with smoothness sufficient, condition for the young to be willing to trade is $q_t^e < \bar{q}$.

Now let us look at the old. Their behaviour is simple: they will want to consume all their endowment of goods and to spend all their money. The old hold all the money there is, which I write as M. Then their consumption demand is given by

$$c_t^O = e_t^O + M/p_t = e_t^O + \bar{M}_t \quad (\bar{M}_t \equiv M/p_t)$$

where the superscript O denotes that the variable refers to the old.

In this little model a rational expectations equilibrium for an economy consisting of a constant population is a sequence of prices and consumption allocations to the young and old such that

$$P_{t+1}^e = P_{t+1} \qquad \text{all } t \qquad (1a)$$

$$c_t^y + c_t^O = e_t^y + e_t^O \qquad \text{all } t \qquad (1b)$$

9

$$c_t^y = \gamma^y(P_{t+1}^e, P_t) \qquad \text{all } t \qquad (1\text{c})$$

$$c_t^O = e_t^O + M/P_t \qquad \text{all } t \qquad (1\text{d})$$

I now turn to a first possibility. We assume that the endowment in the two periods is the same for each generation. This allows us to calculate the $\bar{q}$ which I have already explained. We also notice that, because of condition (1a), we need no longer use the e superscript. Suppose the endowments are such that $\bar{q} < 1$. That means that, in order to induce the young to trade, we need prices to be falling (i.e., $q_t < \bar{q}$). We see from (1d) that the old will have a demand for the good from the young as long as their real cash balances are positive. If prices are falling, real cash balances will be increasing and so the demand of the old will be increasing without bound. But the supply of the good is bounded above by the sum of the endowments. Hence, sooner or later (1b) cannot be satisfied. So this sequence of falling money prices cannot be a rational expectations equilibrium. In fact, it is obvious that the only rational expectations equilibrium that is possible is that of autarky, i.e. the situation where money is worthless – where prices in terms of money are infinite.

So in this case, we see that the infinitely long-lived economy is not enough to yield a monetary economy in rational expectations equilibrium. We get the first whiff of trouble, and in particular the recognition that allowing money to have no other function than being 'a link between the present and the future' is not going to be enough.

In the case that I have just discussed, the only possible rational expectations equilibrium was one in which money has no value. But now we notice something equally unsatisfactory. Whatever the value of the critical $\bar{q}$, the autarky case is always one possible rational expectations equilibrium. So even if other equilibria with a positive exchange value exist, we have no reason to suppose that the economy will be in one of these, rather than in autarky. This is a highly undesirable result. When I first noticed this phenomenon some 15 years ago (Hahn, 1965), I argued that it arose from the fact that we gave money no work to do that could not equally well have been performed by some other asset. This view I still hold, and I shall look at it more carefully presently.

It is worthwhile examining the little model further, for it has some properties that will make Monetarists turn pale.

First let us look at a well behaved case where $\bar{q} > 1$. In that case $q_t = 1$ all t will be rational expectations equilibrium, with a positive exchange value of money. That this is so is easy to see. At $q = 1$ the young will supply some of the good to the old. Moreover, their supply will be quite independent of the real stock of money; that is, it will be independent of the price level. The latter is found to be equating the real stock of money of the old to the given supply of the young at q. The system clearly repeats indefinitely.

Before I proceed, I should notice that this and other results become a little more complicated when the nominal stock of cash is changing. I shall model that a little later without, however, repeating the earlier argument. The following points must be born in mind when modifying the construction in this direction. First, one must decide how the change in the money stock is distributed between generations. Suppose it is always the old who experience this change. Then, second, since we are in rational expectations, it must be the case that the young anticipate the change in their money stock that will occur when they are old. This, third, will now mean that it is no longer the case that the critical $\bar{q}$ will be independent of expected real cash balances. The modifications in the analysis I have given and in the conditions required for the various conclusions can be worked out by anyone who has followed the discussion this far. The same is true if one introduces a changing population.

But now we come to a further disturbing feature: we have not yet exhausted the possible rational expectations equilibria. To see this, let us define Z_t to be the excess demand for the good at date t. From what we already know, we can write

$$Z_t = Z(q_t, \bar{M}_t). \tag{2}$$

If, without change in functional notation, we write this as $Z(P_t, P_{t+1}, M)$, we see that the equilibrium condition

$$Z(P_t, P_{t+1}, M) = 0 \tag{3}$$

constitutes a nonlinear difference equation in prices.

Now suppose endowments and preferences allow the existence of the rational expectations equilibrium $q_t = q^* = 1$ all t, $\bar{M}_t = \bar{M}^* > 0$ all t. Assume also that consumption at the two dates are gross substitutes.[3] Now consider an initial price level such that $\bar{M}_t < \bar{M}^*$. Then the demand of the old will be lower than it would have been. To satisfy (3) we must induce the young to supply less. This by our assumption must mean that they must be faced with less favourable terms of exchanging present for future consumption than those given by q^*. In other words, we must have $q_t > q^*$, so that prices must be rising. But this now means that $\bar{M}_{t+1} < \bar{M}_t < \bar{M}^*$, so that the real stock of cash falls further below its steady-state value. This in turn, by the argument already given, must mean $q_{t+1} > q_t > q^*$ and so on. The economy proceeds in this (accelerating) inflationary mode

[3] In an earlier version I assumed that only consumption goods were normal goods. Azariades objected that this would not suffice for my purposes, but it took Oliver Hart to convince me.

for ever. As time goes to infinity q_t approaches $\bar{q}$ and the real money stock goes to zero. The economy approaches autarky but does not get there in finite time. Since our initial choice of $\bar{M}_t < \bar{M}^*$ was arbitrary, we could have chosen any other initial real money stock below the steady-state one and generated a whole continuum of such rational expectations equilibria. On the other hand, it should be noted that an initial real money stock above its steady-state value is not possible in rational expectations equilibrium; for then q has to be falling below its steady-state value, real balances must be increasing, and the economy will be stopped on its path by the resource constraint.

The equilibria that we have just discovered are bootstrap equilibria (see also Brock and Scheinkman (1980), and Scheinkman (1980)), and they have a family resemblance (no more) to some of the aberrant paths that occur in models of heterogeneous capital goods. But from our present interest they have two notable features. First, we have exhibited a world with rational expectations, inflation and a *constant stock of money*. Next time you read, probably in a letter to *The Times*, that 'a necessary and sufficient condition for inflation is an increasing stock of money', I hope you will remember this simple result. Second, we see that in all of these equilibria the economy is driven towards autarky, i.e. to a state in which money becomes worthless. So once again, while money remains valuable in finite time, it is a precarious and certainly unsatisfactory situation.

Two further points should now be noticed before I proceed to the next step: first, the fully anticipated inflation rate has real effects. This is because that rate gives the terms at which the young can transform present into future consumption and so affects their willingness to trade with the old or, equivalently, to trade. This conclusion will remain valid even if the young can look forward to an augmentation of their money stock when old, provided only that this augmentation is independent of their money transfer.

The second point is connected with the first and concerns the question of money neutrality in these constructions. Let us ignore the autarky equilibrium. The others are defined by a path of relative prices q_t and of real balances $\bar{M}_t$. Suppose that, with constant nominal balances, a stationary equilibrium exists. Then it will be clear that, if the initial nominal stock is changed k-fold, the same stationary equilibrium is possible. If however, nominal balances are changing at the rate of k per cent, the stationary equilibrium will no longer be possible. Under suitable assumptions there will now be a new equilibrium at which money prices are changing at k per cent. In this equilibrium inter-generational trade will be different from what it was in the constant money stock case, and monetary policy will in general have real effects. I emphasize that all agents fully foresee the policy and its effects.

We can make this point more forcibly by showing how monetary policy can be used to avoid equilibrium paths that, with a constant money stock, seek the autarky state.

Suppose that the initial price level exceeds its steady-state value so that at $t = 0$ we have $\bar{M}_0 < \bar{M}^*$. We know that there is a rational expectations equilibrium path with rising prices starting from this initial position, which is asymptotic to autarky. But now consider the policy of taxing or subsidizing the current young when they are old. The tax and subsidy takes the form of taking money away from them or giving them money when they are old. The young, foreseeing this, will change their consumption in the current period. Keeping $q_0 = q^* = 1$, we calculate a linear approximation to this change in the consumption of the young as

$$\Delta c^y = c_w^y (\bar{M}_1 - \bar{M}_0) \qquad (4)$$

where c_w^y is the young's marginal propensity of current consumption out of wealth. Notice that $(\bar{M}_1 - \bar{M}_0)$ is the expected tax or subsidy. For equilibrium we need

$$\Delta c^y + \bar{M}_0 - \bar{M}^* = 0 \tag{5}$$

since $\bar{M}_0 - \bar{M}^*$ is the reduction in demand of the old compared with their steady-state demand. Manipulating (4) and (5), we obtain

$$(\bar{M}_1 - \bar{M}^*) = -\frac{1 - c_w^y}{c_w^y}(\bar{M}_0 - \bar{M}^*).$$

This indeed is the structure of the difference equation for the money stock if the economy is to be in rational expectations equilibrium starting from $\bar{M}_0$ at constant prices ($q_t = q^* = 1$ all t). To be viable we need $(1 - c_w^y)/c_w^y$ sufficiently less than unity. There is no difficulty in finding a class of utility functions that ensure this. The policy then leads to the steady-state real money stock by damped oscillations. Autarky is avoided so the effects are pretty 'real'. It is essential to the argument that money stock changes be fully anticipated. The role of inter-generational distribution effects should also be noted.

Of course, the model that I have been discussing is not only simple – it is downright primitive. We cannot go much further without considering the robustness of our conclusions. In particular, it seems to me peculiar that so many people have been willing to study monetary theory on the basis of a single asset. After all, a central and old problem is to find an explanation for the willingness to hold a 'barren' asset like money when there are fertile ones available. In any case, I shall now introduce another asset into the picture.

It is clear at the outset that, if we want to continue with our model, which gives money no other role than that of facilitating intertemporal substitution, we shall have to make a further far-reaching change in the construction: we shall have to introduce uncertainty. For if not, then either an agent will be indifferent between money and the other asset, or he will hold only one of them. For present purposes, it is easiest to introduce uncertainty into the picture by allowing the endowment of agents to be random variables. More precisely, let S be a set the members of which denote states of the world. Suppose there are a finite number of them. Then the endowments of the young at t and of the old at t are functions defined on S. There is an identically and independently distributed (i.i.d.) probability distribution on S over time, and all of S is in the support of the distribution.

Let us now think of the second asset as government perpetuities; that is, one unit of such a perpetuity is the promise to pay one unit of money for ever. The young are not endowed with this perpetuity. I write P as the price of the good, as before, and β as the price of the perpetuity (or bond). In general, both prices will depend on t and on s, the state of the world. I assume that at t all agents know the state of the world. The actions and plans of the young result from the maximization of expected utility subject to the budget constraints. Thus, the young at t must form an expectation of the price of the bond and the price of the good at $(t + 1)$ for each state s.

The rational expectation hypothesis is now taking the following form: the price of the good and the price of the bond in the *date–event* pair $(t + 1, s)$ that will simultaneously clear both markets in that date–event pair are exactly those that the young at t expected for that date–event pair. And this is true for all t. In other words, *a rational expectations equilibrium* is a pair of functions,

$p(t, s)$, $\beta(t, s)$ such that, when agents maximize their expected utilities at these prices, they take actions that result in the markets for the good and for the bond being in equilibrium at these prices at every date–event pair. A special case of such an equilibrium will be *a stationary rational expectations equilibrium*, where $p(t, s)$ and $\beta(t, s)$ are in fact independent of t and depend only on the state. A further special case is a *quasi-stationary rational expectations equilibrium*, where the price functions take the special form:

$$p(t, s) = h(t) \, p(s), \quad \beta(t, s) = a(t) \, \beta(s).$$

It should be noted that in the definitions I have just given we should think of a state at date t as describing the environment at $(t - 1)$ and at t. Thus, suppose that at any date it is either fine or wet. Then a state is a pair like (fine, wet), (wet, fine), etc., where that is a description of the environment for two adjacent periods. Because of the nature of the overlapping generations models, other histories of the environment are not relevant.

Now let us consider the choice of a young agent in state $\bar{s}$ when the economy is in stationary rational expectations equilibrium. Let us write $g(\bar{s}, s)$ as the gain a young agent who is in state $\bar{s}$ makes on exchanging money for one bond if the state turns out to be s when he is old. This gain is made up of two parts: the interest receipts, and the difference in the price of the bond at s and its price at $\bar{s}$. Notice that we can write the expression for g in this form because by hypothesis both prices are known once s is. Notice also that g can be negative as well as positive. Indeed, if our agent is to hold both bonds and money in $\bar{s}$, then for some s, $g(\bar{s}, s)$ will have to be negative: if not, it would never be expected utility-maximizing to hold money. But now we come up against an important difficulty which, as far as I know, has not been noticed in the literature before. Since there are a finite number of states, and since in a stationary equilibrium the price of bonds depends only on the state, it is possible to designate that state, say $\bar{s}^*$, in which the price of bonds is lowest. That is, $\beta(\bar{s}^*) \leqslant \beta(s)$ all $s \in S$. But then, when $\bar{s} = \bar{s}^*$, none of the young will be prepared to hold any money; for $g(\bar{s}^*, s) > 0$ all s, since the interest payments are positive and one is certain that one cannot make a capital loss. In particular, notice that whatever expectations of the future purchasing power of money the young hold, as long as money has positive exchange value in $\bar{s}^*$ they will prefer to transfer resources by means of bonds rather than money. For the interest on bonds is paid in money, and the price of the good affects the real value of the coupon on bonds in the same way as it affects the real value of money. On the other hand, if the price of money, i.e. its purchasing power, were zero in $\bar{s}^*$ but positive for some s, there would be an unbounded demand for money in state $\bar{s}^*$.

We have thus shown that the model possesses no stationary rational expectations equilibrium. An obvious modification of the details of the arguments show that it possesses no quasi-stationary rational expectations equilibrium either with $a(t)$ increasing in t. In order that in every state there should be a possibility of loss from holding bonds, $a(t)$ would have to be declining in t. In particular, the rate of decline in the worst state $\bar{s}^*$ must exceed $1/\{a(t)\beta(\bar{s}^*)\}$. This immediately shows that the rate of decline must be accelerating, and that the interest rate implicit in that state will be going to plus infinity. Such a quasi-stationary equilibrium, even if it exists, is perhaps not very interesting. There remains the possibility of a non-stationary outcome. Along any realization path it must again be true that at no finite t do we encounter the lowest price of bonds we shall ever encounter. One can see that, once again, there will be no upper bound on the rate of interest along any realization path.

Two remarks are now in order. The fact that there is a state, in the stationary case, at which the price of bonds is at its highest, does not cause similar problems; for while it is then certain that there can be no capital gains from bonds, the possibility that the state will be repeated, and the fact that interest is paid, still makes it possible for some bond-holding to be desirable.

Second, the argument can be made much more general.[4] Suppose there is a continuum of states with the support of bond prices having a non-negative greatest lower bound, say $\underline{\beta}$. Then $\text{prob}(\underline{\beta} \leqslant \beta_{t+1} < \underline{\beta} + 1) > 0$. Now suppose β_t lies in this interval, i.e. in $(\underline{\beta}, \underline{\beta} + 1)$. Then the worse possible outcome from buying a bond at t is $(1 + \underline{\beta})/\beta_t \geqslant 1$, and so in this case no money will be held. Since there is a positive probability that β_t will fall in the stated interval, the argument proceeds as before.

I believe that I have shown that there is something seriously wrong with this way of modelling a monetary economy. If we insist on rational expectations equilibrium, then we had better give money a role that cannot be performed by other assets. This of course, was Keynes's message when he insisted on the superior liquidity of money, although I hasten to add that Keynes was certainly not concerned with rational expectations equilibrium.

One way of going about this is to follow Clower, who imposed the rule that 'only money buys goods'. If we interpret this as meaning that in any one time interval – in any period – an agent can acquire goods only to the value of his money stock, then we can get out of the difficulty that we have just been discussing rather easily. Let agents

---

[4] I owe this argument to Mark Machina. Douglas Gale also made a similar point to me.

Foundations

live for three periods: any agent who transfers assets from the second to the third period will do so only in the form of money, whatever the distribution of the rate of return on bonds. It is easy to see that we have here a route by which rational expectations equilibrium with two valuable assets, one of which is money, can, with some care, be shown to exist.

It is true that this line of argument still seems to leave the possibility of a rational expectations equilibrium in which money has no value – in our example, the case of autarky. But we are now in a position to nail a mistake, which perhaps is best done by modifying the model I have been using to allow for a number of different consumption goods at each date. It is then clear that, while valueless money (it being the only asset) stops inter-generational trade, it does not seem to stop intra-generational trade. But that must now take the form of barter while we have a model of market exchange. In a barter economy, agents must search for partners (think of the 'double-coincidence' argument), and there may now be a role for middlemen where there was none before. Even if the terms at which goods exchange were to be fixed, Ostroy and Starr (1974) have shown that the exchange chain will in general be much longer than that in which every agent meets every other agent once. The mistake that I have referred to consists in continuing to model a barter economy as if it functioned in exchange like a monetary one. It doesn't, and couldn't. Thus the zero exchange value of money equilibria are pseudo-constructs: they are equilibria of a system based on the implicit assumption that the process of exchange proceeds as it does when aided by the device of money. Of course, with proper modelling, we may hope to describe an economy in barter equilibrium – but it is not an equilibrium of the model in which money functions as a medium of exchange. But a little more dramatically, I

20

would argue that, at a zero exchange value of money, there is a sharp discontinuity as the regime – the model – has to be changed. If you include production in your thinking, this conclusion will be even more obvious than it already is. Clower's rule has the virtue that it gives money something to do, and thereby says something about the 'technology' of exchange which is quite absent from the previous model.

But it may now be argued that the Clower procedure assumes what should be explained. For the requirement that only money buys goods is simply a postulate, and one that makes sense only if money indeed has a positive exchange value.

The last point can be met easily. All we need to do is to exhibit an economy constrained in the Clower way in which money does have positive exchange value. I have already indicated how this might be done. But what of the postulate? Here one can proceed in two ways. One can give a theoretical history of how the Clower rule came to be established. This route has been taken by a number of writers (e.g. Hicks, 1969), but I do not for various reasons find the stories that have been told finally convincing or very instructive. The alternative is to start with the institution of fiat money and inquire into the circumstances that make it a stable institution – that is, that allow it to survive. In a sense that is precisely what I have been doing for much of this lecture.

Tobin (1980) has splendidly remarked that money is like language. My speaking English is useful in so far as you do also: just so, money is acceptable to me provided it is acceptable to you. One can think of this argument as a Nash equilibrium. Once there is a rule that transactions should proceed via money, it is not advantageous for an agent to attempt to deviate from this rule. Moreover, the rule ensures its own viability, in the sense that, if it is adhered to, money will have positive exchange value even when there are rival assets, provided we deal with infinitely long-lived economies or with a sensible interpretation of rational expectations equilibrium.

These are rather informal remarks, and they do not amount to a rigorous demonstration that the rule 'only money buys goods' is indeed a social Nash equilibrium. But it is a rule that is, for instance, taken for granted in the literature on the transactions demand for money (Baumol, 1952; Tobin, 1956; and, indeed, most Monetary theorists other than the recent overlapping generations enthusiasts). If it is to serve our purpose, it must be combined with some kind of periodization and/or an appeal to a stochastic process of sales and purchases (Patinkin, 1956). Thus, I have interpreted it as requiring that the value of purchases in any one period cannot exceed the cash available at the beginning of the period; Grandmont and Younes (1972) have interpreted it as meaning that only a fraction of the receipts from sales in any one period can be used for purchases; Tobin and Baumol have models in which receipts and purchases are not synchronized; and Patinkin has suggested that the dates of receipts and purchases are stochastic. In all of this, the question remains of why the periodization is what it is; and, indeed, the determination of dates of receipts and purchases are left rather in the air. Barro (1970) and Clower and Howitt (1975) have to some extent plugged that hole by deriving 'optimum' transaction periods. But certainly this part of the subject is not yet fully settled. It should also be noticed that these theories of transaction demand appeal to a brokerage fee which is incurred in moving between money and other assets.

As a matter of fact, I should now confess that I think the Clower rule is too strong to be shown to be a rule from which there are no departures. Given the rule (and the brokerage fees), there will be terms on which I would accept, say, government bonds for my house. There probably would be some terms on which miners would be indifferent between being paid in money and being paid in coal. We should really be satisfied with the weaker axiom, to the effect that money buys goods *more cheaply* than do other assets. By this I mean that the utility that I can gain by exchanging a given quantity of money for goods at given prices exceeds the utility that I can gain from exchanging assets to an equivalent money value directly for goods. The axiom is meant to capture the comparative disadvantage of direct commodity exchange in an economy where everyone accepts money because everyone else does. Thus, the miner requires more coal than, at the going price, is represented by his money wage if he is to be paid in coal because of the extra costs of converting coal into the goods that he wants. Implicitly, then, we are appealing to transaction's costs.

These are standard arguments, which, alas, does not mean that we have available a formal description of the economy that gives rise to such costs. So far we have got not further than postulating the existence of a 'transactions technology' without linking this in any fundamental way to information requirements. But if we are willing to take that route, then in the small model that I have been using the problems caused by the realization of states in which a positive return on an interest-bearing asset is assured can be overcome. That is, we can find a (stationary) stochastic rational expectations equilibrium for a monetary economy.

The only alternative to this route is to invoke legal arrangements such as the requirement that taxes be paid in money or certain institutional features. Among the latter might be that certain financial assets are not finely divisible (for instance, Treasury bills). Moreover, other real assets, for technological reasons, may also not be finely divisible. It may indeed be the case that the reason for the indivisibility of government debt instruments is precisely to be found in the desire to prevent their monetization. One could imagine co-operative action to overcome this, but this would be costly. (Some of these points are due to Wallace, 1980.)

These are all old problems, and we have not really got much beyond the rather vague notion of the 'non-money-ness' of non-money assets which was used by Hicks (1934). The main point that I have been making is that we cannot do without something like this, we must, in a money asset model, give money a function that differentiates it from other assets as a means of intertemporal substitution. This, as I have argued, is so even when uncertainty is taken into account and we stipulate rational expectations. These matters alert us to the possibility that pure non-interest-bearing money may be under continual pressure. For instance, in America one can now earn interest on current deposits. Computers may reduce the need for a physical medium of exchange to negligibility.

But money, even interest-bearing money or an entry in a computer, needs none the less to be singled out in analysis by virtue of its liquidity. If it were as easy to exchange goods for goods as it is to exchange money for goods, there would be nothing like a monetary economy to study. A surprisingly large number of recent papers that have taken money to be the only means of intertemporal substitution have thereby missed some of the central issues of the subject, quite apart from providing a very unrobust theory, as we have seen. Of course, in practice there may be a number of assets possessed of this superior liquidity – for instance, in Israel the local currency and the dollar seem to function equally as a medium of exchange. There may also be a whole system of assets that are almost as liquid as money itself. But the main point remains: a monetary theory that pays no attentions to liquidity – or, looked at the other way round, which pays no attention to the costs of non-mediated exchange – is not likely to be either robust or useful. As I have already noted, one may in this also appeal to legal and institutional arrangements. Before I leave this topic, let me make the ideas a little more precise. Suppose we live in a world in which everyone who has something to exchange is willing to accept money. We are now (and have been all along) asking what are sufficient conditions for this to be a viable arrangement? One of these is that there should be a finite probability that a seller will not accept anything else in exchange at the terms given by current money prices. If this is true of all sellers but one, then it will also be true of the remaining one. There may be a co-operative way in which, if they all agreed, money could be replaced from, or share, its privileged position. But such co-operation is not possible, or, more precisely, requires a government to bring it about. No single agent can change the situation, although small groups may find ways to economize on money. But we can, I think assume that the smallest self-sufficient group is too large to form.

Consider then a planned exchange of some non-money good or asset for another non-money good or asset. In the light of my argument, even if the terms of their exchange are known, uncertainty is larger for a planned direct exchange than it is for an indirect exchange which goes through money. That is because there is a finite probability of not being able to carry out the direct exchange at the given terms while monetary exchange is certain or more certain. To complete the argument, we now need one further consideration, namely that exchange, even monetary exchange, is costly: the indirect exchange via money to acquire a good or asset costs more than would the single leg from money into the good.

Even in a monetary economy, then, there is an economic niche for the middleman. He reduces or abolishes search costs which would otherwise have to be incurred – indeed, he makes the market of textbook theory. One need only think of the broker, the wholesaler, the retailer and the estate agent to see the point. But mediation uses resources (although fewer than individual search), and so mediation must be paid for.

These ideas can be precisely modelled, and they allow non-money assets to have a positive and sure rate of return without driving out money. Of course, this return must not be too large, and one needs to show that there is indeed a monetary equilibrium in which it is not too large. This can certainly be accomplished in a model in which some transactions are always desirable because, say, the endowments are not sufficiently diversified for each agent. One then wants transaction costs to become large as money balances become small. Casual empirical observation and evidence from hyperinflation do not contradict this hypothesis.

I should note that the notion of liquidity that emerges from this approach in some respects departs from other notions that have been proposed, but also encompasses certain ideas in the literature. Thus I try to separate the speculative from the pure liquidity motive. Keynes does this in discussing the convenience yield of money. Again, the possible delays in finding buyers are included in my formulation under transaction costs; so, with a little care, is the idea that liquidity confers flexibility.

Here is a simple example. Suppose the agent transfers e_1 of good one and e_2 of good two from period 1 to period 2. Because transaction costs put a wedge between buying and selling price, his opportunity set in period 2 is bounded by two straight lines of different slope as in figure 1. If the agent is certain that he would want to consume (e_1, e_2),

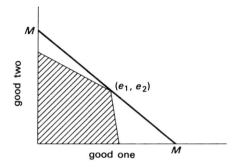

FIGURE 1

then he would be just as happy to transfer these amounts as he would be to hold enough money which puts him on the line *MM*. However, if he is uncertain of his consumption plan, say because he is uncertain of what his preferences will be, then he would clearly prefer to be on *MM*, for then he can vary his trades at a lower penalty in terms of whatever utility function he turns out to have. This is one way in which we can think of flexibility provided by money. This line of argument has been explored by Goldman (1974). Transaction costs play a central role.

They play a central role also in an approach suggested by Foley and Hellwig (1975), who consider a situation where it may at any date be impossible to find a buyer at the going price so that the agent himself can make no exchanges. Holding money is one way of insuring against this. But holding other assets would do as well. Hence, to derive a demand for money balances when there are other assets with sure positive returns again requires transaction costs. These may take the form of uncertainty of finding a buyer for such assets.

Tobin has recently remarked that 'the choices among money, other assets denominated in money, and real capital appear to me central to monetary theory, absent though they are in the overlapping generations model' (1980, p. 88). As usual Tobin is right, and the arguments I have just presented were necessitated by looking this problem in the face. It should be noted that, even in the best of the recent papers on money in overlapping generations, by Wallace (1980), when my assumption of a constant population and money stock are used monetary equilibrium requires there to be a negative rate of return on the only alternative means of intertemporal transfer, namely storage. This is hardly encouraging, and we have seen that uncertainty alone will not get us out of the fix we are in when we resolutely ignore the fact that money is used as a means of exchange.

Kareken and Wallace (1980) object to capturing this role of money by means of the Clower constraint by noting that economic history has examples of a switch from one medium of exchange to another. They therefore conclude that the Clower constraint has not come to grips with fundamentals. From what I have already said, it is clear that I do not disagree with this view, although I have sketched a theory of the medium of exchange role of money, which is a good deal weaker than the Clower constraint. But in a certain sense, I also regard this objection as wrong-headed. We are quite used to the result of game theory that there are many Nash equilibria. Which one we get to is at least partly a matter of history that I have already argued: theorists should not try to construct from first principles. Thus, there may be a perfectly good monetary equilibrium with gold or cowry shells as well as with pound notes. Theory will help only marginally in deciding which it will be. For instance, conquests and wars may be more relevant than economic principles. On the other hand, a change from one medium of exchange to another, say from fiat money to cigarettes, is rather easy to analyse in the framework that I have given.

I now want to conclude this discussion of foundations by some brief remarks on the efficiency of monetary economies. Much that has recently been written on this subject, including I confess by myself (Hahn, 1973a), seems to me now to be rather limited, and a good demonstration of our propensity to be far too serious and sophisticated in models that we can handle but that also happen to miss most of what is interesting. When policy conclusions are drawn from such models, it is time to reach for one's gun.

For an economy without uncertainty which goes on forever, Samuelson (1958), as we all know, made the most important observation on the possible role of money in bringing about a Pareto improvement. This was later elaborated in a splendid paper by Diamond (1965) and an ingenious one by Cass and Yaari (1967), both in the context of optimal growth theory. The point now seems obvious. The creation of money allows the old to trade with the young and allows the old to consume more (of all goods if there are many) than they could under barter. (In my example with a single good the barter equilibrium is autarky.) The young accept the money and thereby allow the old to consume more because they know for certain that the next generation of young will do the same because they in turn know, etc., etc. *ad infinitum*. I have already discussed why we need '*ad infinitum*'. When agents are identical, money allows the existence of an equilibrium that is Pareto-efficient, provided the pre-money equilibrium was not Pareto-efficient already. (In my example, with a constant money stock provided, the exchange rate q was below $\bar{q}$.) When agents are not identical, this conclusion may be false. In the growth context with production, where capital goods are another asset, a steady-state equilibrium requires falling prices if money is to be held. That is because, in these models, money is given nothing to do.

When there is no money, one can find overlapping generations equilibria where the marginal product of capital is below its golden rule value (for the appropriate utility discount rate). This is inefficient for infinitely long-lived economies, since there are feasible paths that will give more consumption to some generations without giving less to others. It occurs because households want to hold more of the only asset there is (capital good) than is production-sensible. The situation is saved by satisfying their asset hunger by creating money for them to hold instead of the capital good. Since there is perfectly anticipated deflation equal to the real rate of interest, households will not care what composition of assets they hold.

Similar ideas emerged when transaction costs are modelled explicitly, still assuming no uncertainty. For reasons that are fully set out elsewhere (Hahn, 1973b), one finds that such costs impose a sequence of budget constraints on the agent. That means that he must satisfy each one of them separately in his plans. Now think of the usual demonstration that a competitive equilibrium is Pareto-efficient. It crucially depends on our being able to show that any Pareto-superior allocation will not be budget-feasible for some agents and not in the interior of the budget for any and hence not physically feasible. This requires a single budget constraint. Starrett (1973) gave specific examples of how in the sequence case the equilibrium failed to be Pareto-efficient. If into this picture we introduce money, then it becomes possible for the individual to make his plans as if there were only one budget constraint; for he can now, in any one period, spend more than he earns from selling his goods. In order for this to work, Starrett and I assumed that, at the end of his life, the agent must return all the money he has at the beginning. It is easy to see that in equilibrium there will now be discount factors, given by the marginal rates of substitution between money at different dates, which will be the same for all agents such that the agent acts as if he maximized utility subject to the constraint that the present value of his purchases is equal to the present value of his sales. I called such an economy an 'inessential sequence economy', and it has all the efficiency properties of an Arrow–Debreu economy without any uncertainty. Money here allows the breaking of the barter *quid pro quo*, which is imposed by a lack of trust for which money is now a substitute. In a profound paper, Douglas Gale (1978) has shown how this function of money is essential if the core of a sequence economy – the sequential core – is not to be empty.

But all this leaves uncertainty out of account. When we again formulate an economy where important parameters are functions of a random state of nature, and where no (or too few) contingent future contracts are possible, we seem to be in trouble. For there will now be a budget constraint for each date–event pair, and it is not clear that the device of money will lead to their amalgamation. The decisive work here is by Bewley (1980). He shows how, in an economy of infinitely long-lived agents, money can provide not only the means of intertemporal transfer, but also the means of self-insurance, that is, a substitute for contingent futures markets. He proves the remarkable result that, under certain circumstances, such an economy does as well as one with a full complement of markets. Unfortunately, it seems to me that infinitely long-lived agents are essential to this story. In less demanding contexts, we would need as many different monetary assets as there are states of nature to achieve this result.

In fact, any model that is even mildly descriptive of an actual economy will not be Pareto-efficient in the Arrow–Debreu sense. This observation may lead one to a different approach to efficiency. We look at the equilibrium of the model that we have constructed with at least one eye on

31

the world. We then ask: what would the feasible allocation set have to look like in order for this equilibrium to be efficient? It would contain features that recognize certain institutional restrictions and, for instance, the impossibility of reallocating goods across states. When we have done that, we could say that the economy has been characterized. Drèze (1974) and Grossman and Hart (1979) have done this. One can then ask whether this characterization is based on the true feasibility set for society, and can draw conclusions accordingly. As far as I know, this has not been done by anyone except perhaps in the discussions of the optimum quantity of money.

So the question of the efficiency of an economy that can accommodate money and other assets leads to quite new directions. And I have not yet even discussed production – in fact, a large majority of the efficiency discussions for a monetary economy are carried out for a world of pure exchange. When there is production *and* the missing markets we need for monetary theory, all hell is let loose. For one thing, it no longer is at all clear what the firms' objectives should be since they are owned by shareholders whose marginal rates of substitution of wealth across states will, in general, differ. Certain answers have been obtained by brute force, and a use of false conjectures by agents (e.g. Grossman and Hart). There are also some answers for large economies (Hart, 1979). But for what might look a little like actual economies, we have nothing on offer.

I return to this and other problems with a production economy in the next lecture. Here I want to conclude with an equally important reason why the fastidious economist should not pay too much attention to the current mode of analysing the superiority of a monetary over a barter economy.

It seems obvious to me that the existence of money makes it more profitable to engage in production for exchange, and that this in turn allows, as Smith noted some time ago, a finer division of labour than would occur under barter. Not only will money allow a wider variety of goods to be traded, but it will also allow the exploitation of increasing returns which are so notably absent from much of our analysis. At its weakest, it will become worthwhile to provide skills that were not usefully acquired under barter. All this needs to be properly formalized. Until that is done, results on the comparative efficiency of barter and money economies are not of much use. More importantly, their methodology is at fault when they keep the feasible set unchanged when passing from a barter to a monetary economy. As I have already said, some of the very essentials of the story are missing in these exercises.

II

Money and the Real Economy

Towards the end of my last lecture, I made some comparison between a barter and a monetary economy. The somewhat familiar arguments that I used there are, it seems to me, quite sufficient to convince one that there are profound real differences between a barter and a monetary economy. Even though the world is full of models that suggest otherwise, I do not want to pursue the obvious any further. Instead, I shall now be concerned only with monetary economies; that is, with economies in which we can be certain that money always has a positive exchange value. I want to study how such economies are affected by changes in monetary aggregates.

Let us begin with an axiom that I think most economists would accept, and that I have already used in the previous lecture: the objectives of agents that determine their actions and plans do not depend on any nominal magnitudes. Agents care only about 'real' things, such as goods (properly dated and distinguished by states of nature), leisure and effort. We know this as the axiom of the absence of money illusion, which it seems impossible to abandon in any sensible analysis. Care must, however, be taken not to allow the axiom to rule out the possibility that an agent makes mistakes. That is, the axiom does not

34

rule out situations where purely nominal changes are mistakenly, but rationally, perceived as real.

In recent years this axiom has been combined with the notion of rational expectations to lead to the conclusion that changes in monetary aggregate can mainly affect the real economy if they lead agents to confuse nominal with real changes. For instance, it has led economists like Lucas (Lucas and Rapping, 1969) to propose a theory that points to the view that our present unemployment is to be explained by the mistaken, but rationally formed, belief of workers that the normal real wage has not fallen. They are, it is argued, substituting present for future leisure. Since, contrary to what one might have thought, this view is widely held to be correct, indeed is endorsed by powerful politicians, who conclude that they either cannot or ought not to do anything about unemployment, it is clear that the subject we are about to examine is of some practical importance. Lucas is the intellectual leader of this approach, which I shall refer to as Lucasian. One might also call it Monetarist, except that economists who use this label are not given to the precision of Lucas.

I shall want to argue that these quite peculiar, and to me counter-intuitive and counterfactual, conclusions are not entailed by the fundamental axiom, or indeed by the assumption that, in forming their expectations, agents use all the information available to them. The contrary belief is due partly to the circumstance that macroeconomists of this school pay insufficient attention to the richness of their own model. More importantly, however, I want to argue that the model is seriously incomplete, and that its descriptive status must be in doubt. At the level of rigour and generality of existing Lucasian models, I shall propose a theory that does not yield Lucasian results. I shall claim that that theory has at least as much claim on our attention as does the Lucasian.

First, however, there is one point to be got out of the way. There are now quite a few econometric studies of Lucasian (and Monetarist) models available, and some of them do not contradict the proposed theory. No test, as far as I know, has been performed on comparative models on the lines discussed by Deaton and Pesaran (1978). The rather sharp conflict between the theory and the social and political consequences of unemployment has not been studied. Evidence of fruitless job search and of job queues in, say, the 1930s, has not been looked at. Much of the econometrics turns on the supply of undifferentiated labour hours and the rather odd belief that, for the economy, one can meaningfully speak of the supply curve of such hours. No evidence of unionized labour sectors has been used (at least, not by Lucas and Rapping, 1969). In short, I hold the view that such econometric evidence as there is is tenuous. Some of this empirical work is interesting, and I do not wish to argue that it is worthless; it is, however, a long way from being conclusive. The field is wide open for thorough theoretical investigation.

I shall now proceed by a number of steps. The first considers the Lucasian propositions. I will not, however, follow Lucas into his special island model (1972), nor shall I ask you to consider three or four log-linear macro-equations plucked from a microeconomic textbook and aggregated by faith and determination. The aim will be to maintain contact with serious theory.

Suppose, once again, and of course provisionally, that the only transferable asset is money. Suppose also, to begin with, that agents can distinguish every state of nature from every other, and that they can observe states directly. In the Lucasian world the market opportunities for transactions in date–event pair (t, s) depend only on prices and endowments at that date–event pair. The endowment of goods is a random variable depending on the state and date. For the moment, however, the endowment of money is exactly what has been transferred from the previous period. The present is given by the pair $(0, \bar{s})$ and, unlike our earlier simple model, we assume the agent to be ·endowed with a stock of money at the beginning of the present. Also in the present, the agent forms expectations of prices for future date–event pairs. For simplicity, we shall assume that, while an agent is uncertain about future states, his expected prices are single valued functions of the date–event pair. The expectations are formed rationally: that is, the agent uses all the information available to him.

The agent's preferences are defined over his consumption bundle in each date–event pair. Consumption here includes the consumption of leisures. For the present, let us look at pure exchange; I shall have a good deal to say about production later. The agent chooses a policy in the light of his present and expected market opportunities. A policy determines transactions, and hence consumption, for each date–event pair including the present. The policy results from standard maximizing behaviour, and I assume that it is unique.

If we do not explicitly model a transaction demand for money and consider, for simplicity, a finitely-lived economy, then we know that we shall have to introduce some feature to ensure a positive exchange value of money. For my present purpose this can be quite crude, and I shall stipulate that, at the end of the final period, all the money stock that there is must be returned to the authorities. In particular, each agent must then return the money stock he had at the beginning plus any increments (positive or negative) in this stock that he might receive from the authorities subsequently. The assumption, of course, is not to be taken literally – it is made here to allow me to proceed with an argument that interests me.

In this economy, a rational expectations equilibrium is a

function from date–event pairs to prices which represents the theory of the agents and which is consistent with market-clearing at each date–event pair when agents have optimal policies relatively to their theory, expectations and endowments. The basic axiom now tells us that, if the initial money stock of each agent is multiplied by a positive scalar k, then multiplying all equilibrium prices by k will again be a rational expectations equilibrium. Hence the set of equilibrium consumption allocations is invariant under the multiplication of every agent's initial money stock by k. This, however, is not yet the famous neutrality of money proposition of the textbooks. For that claims that the set of equilibrium relative prices is invariant under the multiplication of the *total* initial money stock by k. This will be the case if all agents are alike in the sense of Gorman (1953); that is, if all agents have parallel linear Engel curves through the origin. I should here remark that this is never so in my overlapping generations model if the young are endowed with money since the demand for money by the old is identically zero. This assuming away of distributional matters is not harmless.

Sometimes one comes across the claim that distributional real consequences of a k-fold change in the total initial money stock may indeed affect relative prices, but only transitorily. That is, it is claimed that for every ϵ, there is a T such that, on a proper measure, the distance between the equilibrium sets of relative prices and consumption allocations in the two economies is less than ϵ for all time periods after T. Except for trivial cases, I have not seen a proof of this claim.

But we shall now see that assuming away distributional matters will, in this model, have fatal consequences. For now the price level is in fact indeterminate. The reason for this is as follows. When Gorman assumptions are made, then the economy behaves as if there were only a single agent who has all the economy's endowment. Call this the fictional economy. The equilibrium of this economy occurs when prices are such that the single agent in each date–event pair just wants to consume all the goods he owns and hold all the money he has. If all these prices are multiplied by k, the same consumption plan remains feasible for this agent. He can also meet his money obligations in the last period. All terms of trade are what they were before. Hence the fictional economy is still in equilibrium when all prices are multiplied by k and the money stock is constant. It is instructive to recall at this stage how the distribution effects between young and old in the overlapping generations model serve to prohibit this kind of conclusion.

One might now seek to avoid these difficulties by introducing transaction constraints of the Clower variety which I have already discussed. However, then, even if the Gorman conditions on preferences are met, these constraints will in general be a source of distribution effects if in any equilibrium they are biting constraints. If they are not biting, then we are still where we were.

I therefore conclude that no economy that is isomorphic to the fictional economy can be the basis of interesting monetary theory. From this, it follows that a claim that, if agents know for sure what the behaviour of the total money stock will be, the real equilibria of the economy will be invariant to this behaviour, is false. Agents, in a proper model, will also have to know the distribution of the money stock in each date–event pair. This conclusion, I believe, is not of minor theoretical or practical importance.

Let us now take the next step. Suppose that every agent in an economy that is in rational expectations equilibrium is informed at the present that their money stock from date T onwards will be k times what it is in the prevailing equilibrium. We can argue as follows. When date T arrives all agents will, except for money, have the same endowment in every state that they would have had in the old equilibrium. That is so because money is the only means of intertemporal transfer. Hence if we multiply all former equilibrium prices for T and later by k, we will again have a rational expectations equilibrium from T onwards. But what of the prices before date T? If they remain at their old values the terms of trade between goods at date–event pairs before T and goods at date–event pairs at and after T will be different from what they were in the old equilibrium. If we had the Gorman conditions and no transactions constraint, the answers would then be that all equilibrium prices before T would also be multiplied by k. But we already know that this move in the game leads to disaster.

Without these assumptions, one cannot rigorously deduce anything definite about the new price level before T, if for no other reason than that there are no grounds for believing that relative prices before T will remain at their old equilibrium values. Certainly, if all prices before T were k times their previous value, then agents who had planned to consume some of their money before T will experience real effects which will not be cancelled by the real effects of those who were planning to accumulate money. Moreover, if there are biting transaction constraints and k is close to one, this will be another source of real effects. On the other hand, the prospect of the k-fold change in prices from T onwards will have an effect on agent's accumulation plans before T. Collectively, of course, they cannot accumulate more money than there is, and for equilibrium they cannot accumulate less, either.

If, to be specific, k is greater than one, then there will be a tendency for the new equilibrium prices in terms of money to be higher than they were at dates before T. This will affect the transactions that can be carried out as well

40

as the transactions that are desired. There is every reason to suppose that relative prices will be different from what they were.

In a well formulated model, therefore, fully anticipated money stock changes have real effects. I have already given an example of this in the previous lecture. But we must now note that we have vastly underestimated these real effects of our experiment by insisting that money is the only link between the present and the future. If, for instance, goods are storable, we can no longer conclude that what happens from T onwards is independent of what happened before – indeed, the whole method of analysis I have used so far breaks down. All one can say is that the new equilibrium may in real terms differ from the old not only before T but afterwards as well.

It is probably for this reason that in the literature so much attention has been focused on steady states. They do not properly belong here where the model excludes production and the economy is of finite duration. I shall however, discuss them briefly later (p. 47). But I note here that calculations in proposed models have shown convergence times to steady state to be very long indeed (Atkinson, 1969).

So far, then, the situation is this: neglecting distributional effects yields neutrality of the total current money stock but also makes the price level indeterminate unless some new feature is introduced into the model. If that is a Clower-like transaction constraint, then in general there will be distribution effects and the only safe proposition is that money is neutral under equi-proportionate changes in each agent's initial money stock. Future money in general is not neutral. It will be obvious that these results on their own are without causal significance: for that one would need to postulate that rational expectations equilibrium is unique and that the economy is always in rational expecta-

41

tions equilibrium, which is a matter of faith and not of science.

Before we take the next step, I should like to make two points.

It is clear that those macroeconomists in the new fashion who have retained contact with elementary theory are aware of distribution effects although they may not have thought through the logical implications of their absence. For some reason, however, they equally clearly regard them as either small or of short duration. I am at a loss to understand their warrant for these beliefs. If the rest of economic theory proceeded on these assumptions, welfare economics, for instance, would become extremely simple and stability analysis would be child's play. Indeed, a competitive economy could always be studied as if it were maximizing a utility function. Much of what we have regarded as interesting and important would be lost. On the other hand, let us agree that in models as general as the present one nothing very systematic, let alone of macroeconomic interest, can be said about the distribution effects: to do that one will need a model with more structure – for instance the overlapping generations model.

The second point is slightly more technical, and I make it to prevent confusions that might arise between the foregoing analysis and the quite different proposition that, in the present model, the price level in all final date–event pairs is indeterminate. This will be true without any special distributional assumptions, and implies that the economy has a continuum of equilibria. The proposition follows when we recall that the aggregate demand for money in the final period must be independent of the price level in the final period. For this aggregate demand is determined by the requirement that all money balances be returned to the authorities. Hence in the final period Say's law applies: the value of the excess demand *for goods* is identically zero. The rest follows. It is of course true only because of the artefact of the model with its requirement that all money be returned. I am rather doubtful that it points to any real phenomenon.

We now take the next step. The neutrality of money propositions, both true ones and false ones, when mixed with rational expectations, have proved to be a heady mixture. The journals are full of claims that monetary policy must be ineffective or, if it is effective, is so only because it cannot be predicted. There are also many papers with more or less ingenious reasons why money may not be as neutral as all that anyway. The rather obvious point – that agents would, in general, have to know the distribution of the money stock for us to be able to derive ineffectiveness propositions – is never, to my knowledge, made. The equally obvious point, that current announcements of future money changes can have real effects, seems to have been ignored. Much of the source of this feverish activity is Lucas's splendid paper of 1972. It is splendid because it brilliantly illuminates an important theoretical point. It is also disastrous, both to Lucas himself and to others, because it has led him and them to believe that this was the only point in need of illumination.

The problem that Lucas perceived was this. In his presidential address to the American Economic Association, Friedman (1968) had given a clear exposition of the neutrality doctrine: 'the unimportance of money', as he called it. Yet he also advocated as a matter of urgency specific rules for the control of the money supply. For Friedman there was no contradiction: he was sufficiently pragmatic to recognize that there would be real effects as the economy adjusted to monetary shocks. To avoid real effects, one must avoid monetary shocks, that is unforeseen changes in the money stock. Lucas set out to make these propositions precise and thus discussable.

I am sure that the essentials of this story are well known and that I can be brief. The general aspect can be seen as follows. Suppose the stock of money is fixed and known to everyone. Let s_1 and s_2 be the only two states which the economy can be in at time t. Assume that one group of agents always knows which of the two states obtains while the other does not. If market-clearing prices are different in the two states, then the uninformed can deduce the state from the prices. If an equilibrium therefore exists, both groups will be equally well informed – the ignorant obtaining their information from prices. In general for this case, such a 'fully revealing' equilibrium exists. Now change the story, so that at date t there is a random and unobserved augmentation of the money stock of ΔM. Then the market-clearing prices for s_1 with $\Delta M = 0$ may be the same as for s_2 with some $\Delta M \neq 0$. Prices no longer reveal the state to the uninformed. Doing the best they can, they will make mistakes in judging the state of the economy. Evidently the random ΔM has real effects.

As an example, suppose workers' marginal productivity is higher in state s_1 than it is in state s_2 for any employment level. Employers know the state but workers do not. Moreover, workers observe only their current wage and last period's prices. With some assumptions, and without monetary disturbance, this can be made consistent with a fully revealing equilibrium. With monetary disturbance, however, workers cannot deduce accurately whether, say, a higher money wage today indicates the higher productivity state s_1, or whether their productivity is still as given by s_2 but there has been a monetary injection. Since they must give some credence to s_1 obtaining, their supply of labour increases. The employers are willing to hire them even if state s_2 is the true one because they know that the prices of goods will be higher in a greater proportion than money wages are. Before you know where you are, you have a Phillips curve and it is entirely generated by monetary noise.

Lucas's contribution then is this. He showed how unpredictability or unobservability of monetary policy could interfere with the information-revealing function of prices, and how this could be the source not only of real effects, but of real effects that the macro-literature had noted. He thereby reconciled real effects from monetary events with neutrality propositions and with rational expectations. I do not, however, find that he has committed himself to the view that fully anticipated monetary changes have no real effects – that has become a dogma only with some of his excitable followers.

The time has now come to stop and to survey the scene. It is, it seems to me, an extremely peculiar one. We are in a world where some of the most urgent concerns of public policy can find no place. At every moment and in every state, everyone who wants to work at the going real wage is doing so. The employment offered depends only on prices – current and expected – and has nothing whatsoever to do with the forecast demand for output at these prices. Fluctuations in output and employment may occur even with a perfectly predictable monetary policy. But such fluctuations reflect the succession of states. It is true that recently, in a fascinating paper, Azariadis (1980) has shown how an economy can have such fluctuations in rational expectations equilibrium by conditioning expectations on irrelevant aspects of otherwise identical states, such as sunspots. But for the Lucasians and the Monetarists, the states are real and relevant. All unnecessary fluctuations are due to the erratic behaviour of the authorities. Not only is systematic monetary policy ineffective, but also there is no ground for any sane government to pursue such, or indeed any other, macro-policy. Rational expectations equilibria are unique and the economy is always in rational expectations equilibrium. Appearances belie reality. Firms expensively engaged in forecasting the demand for, say, motor cars are really forming price expectations. Workers complaining of lack of jobs are really complaining about the low wage they are being offered in readily available ones. Economics, being the subject it is, cannot easily refute all this. But there certainly is sufficient ground for thinking again.

The second leg of this discussion accordingly explores whether there is any escape from the embrace of the Lucasians and the Monetarists: by this I mean whether there are not properly formulated theories that do not have such implausible implications. As before, I shall proceed by a series of steps.

Let us start with an example that sticks closely to the Lucasian Walrasian world. However, for the moment I abstract from uncertainty and allow production. It will be clear at the end how stochastic features could be introduced into the story without affecting the main conclusions. I shall assume production conditions that are consistent with the dynamic non-substitution theorem (Mirrlees, 1969). I assume that this theorem is well known, and only remind you that it postulates universal constant returns to scale, no joint production other than that involved by the transfer of capital goods of one date to (used) capital goods at the next date, non-shiftable capital goods between sectors, and one non-produced input, here labour, which is essential to production. For any given rate of profit or interest in a given interval, the theorem tells us that there will be a unique vector of goods prices in terms of labour depending on that rate which is consistent with steady-state equilibrium. I follow the Monetarists in assuming that each agents' linear Engel curve through the origin is parallel to that of any other agent. I assume, again as many Monetarists do, that the demand for cash balances

46

is, for transactions reasons, proportional to the value of gross output. Lastly, for simplicity we look at the zero growth case so that the rate of interest is such as to induce households to make zero net additions to their assets. Again this is quite inessential.

Now, if in this economy the supply of labour is perfectly elastic at the real wage determined by the steady-state interest rate, then it is easily checked that there will be a continuum of steady-state equilibria all with different levels of employment, output and real balances. Of course, actual transition from one of these equilibria to another may be complicated and unsure; but we may take a leaf out of the Monetarist book and assume that it takes place smoothly.

We start in steady-state equilibrium. Now let the money stock be *k* per cent higher. The axiom applies so that, if all money prices are *k* per cent higher, we are again in equilibrium. But suppose money prices are constant and gross output is *k* per cent higher: then the demand for money and goods will be *k* per cent higher. Moreover, ignoring the transition, the entitlement to interest payments will be *k* per cent higher. So that too is a steady-state equilibrium. Therefore anyone living in this economy and persuaded by the Monetarists that the transition to steady state is rapid enough to be ignored is in a quandary. He observes the money stock to be *k* per cent higher. A rational expectation is that all prices will be *k* per cent higher. But it is also a rational expectation that output will be *k* per cent higher. If he has been reading the *Journal of Political Economy* and Minford, he and others may opt for the first hypothesis, if he is a faithful Keynesian, for the second. To be really rational, he would have to know what his fellow citizens have been reading. In any case if the higher money stock does go with higher prices, it could be argued that is so because the Monetarists have talked everyone into believing that it will. Certainly, money could be pretty non-neutral in this economy.

Now this example is somewhat extreme, although close relatives may be found in much of the growth literature. I shall not put it forward as of descriptive significance. I do put it forward to show that the new macroeconomists have taken far too limited a view of the Neoclassical model and have been somewhat blinded by what is, after all, a banal axiom. Not only can the basic model yield multiple equilibria (it does so very often), but, from my point of view more importantly, it may require agents to make quantity predictions. Thus, under constant returns to scale, firms must know not only prices but what will be sold. But in fact this conclusion goes beyond constant returns. Thus a household owner of a share in a firm does not know his entitlement to profit if he knows only prices: he needs to know the profit function of the firm, which is equivalent to knowing the production plan of the firm at the given prices. So it is not true that even in the most traditional models market opportunities are fully described by prices. The example I have considered has at least this virtue: it is consistent with the observation that most firms are anxious to forecast demand at given prices.

Before I take this hint and move away from perfect competition Walrasian constructions altogether, I want, still in the more traditional framework, to look more closely at a Lucasian black box.

When Lucasians postulate that prices are 'flexible' they seem to mean that we can observe only Walrasian market-clearing prices. There is no nonsense here about the invisible hand doing any noticeable and comprehensible work: its task is accomplished by definition. So right at the centre of the argument there seems to be a gaping void. One may agree with Lucas's methodological reflection that economic theory can deal only with equilibrium, that is rational, actions and still acknowledge ample room for doubt concerning Lucasian definitions of price flexibility. It will be seen that I am in Lucas's methodological spirit when, instead, I propose that prices are flexible when there are no obstacles to price change when it is to someone's advantage to do so. More formally, prices in a given theory are flexible when their formation is endogenous to the theory. In this way one avoids a tautological confidence trick exposed by the following exchange: 'Involuntary unemployment is due to wages not being flexible.' 'How so?' 'Because I say that wages are flexible when there is no involuntary unemployment.'

Now as a matter of fact, prices in the Lucasian world are not properly endogenous to the fundamental theory, because there is no theory of the actions of agents that explains how prices come to be such as to clear Walrasian markets. It is an article of faith that they always do so, or, perhaps less pejoratively, an axiom. But I do not find it helpful to have a central problem of economic theory, and indeed of economic policy, treated in this way. However, I also readily admit that it is easier to live by faith, and that at the moment a fully worked out theory of price (and wage) formation is not to be had. So what I shall now have to say will be somewhat primitive and partial, and one hopes that it will soon be made obsolete by further work.

Let us return to the constant returns economy I have already discussed, with this alteration: at the substitution theorem real wage there is involuntary unemployment. Lucas has said that he finds this a mysterious notion, but in fact it is crystal clear: the shadow real wage of the unemployed is below the prevailing real wage.[1] That is what I think Keynes had in mind, but in any case it is

---

[1] The shadow wage is that wage which, when paid to an employed person, would yield him the same utility as that which he obtains when unemployed.

plain that that is what every theorist must mean. The situation then is one in which some agents find that they cannot sell their labour. In a more elaborate context, we could say that the probability of getting a job is less than one and that workers would be willing to pay to have that probability higher than it is.

What I think Lucas must really mean is not that involuntary unemployment cannot be precisely defined, but that it is impossible in a world of rational agents. On this I shall have a good deal to say later on, but here I should like to note that on my (and Keynes's) definition this view would have to be false. For the rational agent may choose not to accept a job that is available at a considerably lower wage and yet his shadow wage may be less than the prevailing market rate. Or suppose you are an unemployed professor and you can get a job as an advisor to Mrs Thatcher. You may be perfectly willing to work rationally as a professor at a wage less than that prevailing for this group, without being willing to move to 10 Downing Street. As a professor you are involuntarily unemployed. Again, the reduction in wage I would have to accept to get a job at the University of Chicago may exceed the difference between the prevailing wage there and my shadow wage. But I am an involuntary unemployed Chicago economist. I emphasize: we are inerested not in the 'true' meaning of 'involuntary' but in the definition of a technical term which seems rather obviously useful for analysis.

The recent proposed theories of implicit labour contracts require one modification of the proposed definition: a worker is involuntarily unemployed if the expected utility of prevailing contracts exceeds his utility when unemployed. An involuntarily unemployed worker is thus not a 'laid off' worker but one without a contract that he would be willing to accept at terms worse (in utility) than are prevailing.

Now the situation is what it is because money wages and prices are too high so that real cash balances are too low. I make this assumption in order to keep close to the Lucasians and not because I consider this to be the only, or indeed the most important, explanation of involuntary unemployment. Time is a device that stops everything happening at once, and I do not consider it necessary to argue that such states as I am postulating could at least momentarily exist, for instance because of an unforeseen shock. The contrary view probably involves horrendous philosophical problems with causality, which I leave to others.

The real question is: what happens next? For the present I intend to be quite orthodox and suppose that the state cannot persist and that money wages and prices will begin to fall. One would like to tell a story of such prices changes based on the rational calculation of agents. I share Friedman's view that in our present state of knowledge this is not possible for even mildly general models. But for my purposes I need agreement on only one point, and that is that full Walrasian equilibrium need not be reached by a single step. I am at present quite willing to suppose that such an equilibrium will be reached by a finite number of steps.

Now, even if agents know what the full Walrasian equilibrium prices are, it may not be in the interest of anyone to declare his willingness to trade at the appropriate equilibrium price at the first step. I have it in mind, of course, that there are steps – that is, that an agent does not change prices continuously because it simply takes time to recognize and to process signals, and because a single step might not be advantageous. In fact, agents will be participating in a sequential game which, however, is not co-operative. The unemployed agent, under present assumptions, correctly calculates that a very small reduction in the wage at which he is willing to work will suffice to get him employed provided others have not done the same. In any case, his own actions will crucially depend on the actions of others. It is true that, if at the first step everyone else sets the Walrasian price, then he cannot do better than do likewise. It is one possibility and one solution to the game, but it is unlikely to be the only one.

Nothing very revolutionary is here being proposed. There is a vast, if not very satisfactory, literature on processes by which a Walrasian equilibrium may come to be established. It is quite a novel proposition that nothing but Walrasian equilibrium can ever be observed. If then it is granted that there will be a real process in real time which for the sake of the present argument does lead the economy to a Walrasian equilibrium, then we can also make the following simple point: if the stock of money is increased so that, ignoring distribution effects, it would at the existing money price and wages yield the Walrasian real cash balances, then equilibrium could be achieved in one step without any prices having to change at all. It is of the essence for this argument that agents anticipate the increase in the money stock; for in doing so, constant returns producers will correctly anticipate that they can sell more at the going prices. That is, there is a rational expectations single-step constant-price path to full equilibrium.

One now notices that, if all agents are in thrall to the Monetarists, the expectation of the augmented money stock might cause them all to mark up prices in the proportion in which the money stock has increased; that is, they refuse to budge from the price and quantity adjustment path to equilibrium that would have taken place anyway. The monetary change is ineffective because it has no effect on the adjustment path. Once again, one sees that there is in fact more than one outcome consistent with rationality.

At this level of informality, one must not claim too much, so let me make the minimal claim. First, the model shows that, starting out of Walrasian equilibrium, the fundamental axiom and rationality are perfectly consistent with prices remaining constant with a perfectly anticipated increase in the money stock. In fact, it is consistent with a Keynesian view. Since Keynes did not use the further Lucasian axiom that involuntary unemployment was impossible, this is not perhaps surprising. Second, the argument strongly suggests – I cannot alas put it more strongly – that adjustment paths to Walrasian equilibrium can in real terms be affected by changes in the money stock. This is because, in this model, agents form quantity expectations, and there is a rational path to equilibrium at constant prices when the money stock is appropriate changed. There is no such path with a constant money stock, and there is no Nash-like path which could be generated by agents supposing that other agents keep their prices unchanged. Accordingly, unless we suppose that agents always find it rational to change their prices in the same proportion – and I cannot exclude that – the constant money stock path will differ in real terms from the other.

Now this second conclusion has been challenged by McCallum (1980), who has constructed a macro-model to show that, even in the situation that I am discussing, systematic monetary policy would be ineffective; that is, the path of real variables is independent of this policy. Although he writes down a number of equations, they are not needed to make his point. He assumes that real wages are constant throughout, so that all prices of all goods always change in the same proportion as do money wages, and one can unambiguously speak of a price level. He then assumes that if, say, the money stock increases by k per cent, the fall in the price level that would otherwise have taken place because of involuntary unemployment will be *k* per cent less. Hence the real cash balances at any date will be exactly what they would have been anyway, and so the real evolution of the economy is unaffected. The assumption is justified as follows (I assume). When the money stock increases by *k* per cent, then agents deduce that the Walrasian equilibrium price level will be *k* per cent higher and so are aware that *pro tanto* lower reductions in money wages will get them where they want to be. In this the agents act myopically – knowing the money policy, they make no attempt to calculate the ultimate Walrasian price level.

This construction seems to me to highlight much that is wrong with recent macroeconomics. Much importance is attached to rationality until it comes to price changes: then anything goes. For the Lucasians, prices change to keep Walrasian markets cleared by a mechanism that is entirely secret in the Lucasian mind. For McCallum, the mode of price change is such as to give him the result that he seeks. But consider just the following simple point. The unemployed know that, whatever they do, the real wage will remain unchanged. McCallum gives no reason for the sequential nature of price changes. But like everything else, they should be the outcome of the calculations of agents. Until that has been analysed, we cannot judge whether even fully anticipated monetary changes present otherwise unavailable real options. For instance, to take the crudest case: if nominal price changes are costly, then monetary changes, by making it possible to economize on such changes, gives new real options. Of course, I am reasonably supposing that changes in monetary aggregates involve lower costs.

But let me look at a very simple model to make this point. It will also serve to introduce the next stage in the argument.

To lend some mild realism, I assume that there are two kinds of workers, type 1 and type 2, who between them produce one composite good. Production takes one period and the price of the good at t is given by

$$p_t = c\{w_1(t - 1), \; w_2(t - 1)\}$$

where c is the unit cost function, $w_i(t)$ the money wage of type i and p_t the money price of the good. There are thus constant returns to scale. The wage is paid at the beginning of the period and I assume a zero interest rate. Competition ensures zero profits. As long as they can get the labour, firms will be willing to supply whatever is demanded at these prices, and I assume that they forecast demand perfectly. The demand for the good is given by the Monetarist equation which makes it proportional to real cash balances. The demand for each type of labour at t is thus a function, through the price equation, of the wage rates at (t) and the stock of cash at $(t + 1)$. Similarly, $\bar{w}_i(t)$, the real wage paid at t for type i, is a function of the wage rates of the previous period and the current wage $w_i(t)$. I shall write $n_i(t)$ as the number of type i employed at t expressed as a fraction of all those of type i willing to work at t. It also depends on the wage rates at t and $(t - 1)$ and cash balances at $(t + 1)$. Of course, n_i can never exceed unity.

The story starts with $n_i < 1$ at $t = 1$ for both types. I now make two assumptions: first, that it is labour that sets the money wage, and second, that type 1 can change its money wage only at odd dates and type 2 only at even dates. The last assumption attempts, in a rather crude but not too unrealistic way, to capture the fact that workers cannot co-ordinate their wage changes. The other assumption is a first approximation, and I return to it below.

I now stipulate that each type's behaviour can be rationalized by the hypothesis that they are out to maximize:

$$\sum_t U^i\{\bar{w}_i(t), n_i(t)\} \, d^t$$

where $d < 1$ and U^i is monotone increasing in both arguments over their range of definition. If we use what has already been argued, we can write this expression more fully as

$$\sum_t U^i[\bar{w}_i\{w(t-1), w(t)\}, \quad n_i\{m_{t+1}, w(t-1), w(t)\}] \, d^t$$

where $w(t)$ is the vector of money wages at t, m_t the stock of cash at t.

We can now set down a number of fairly transparent observations on the situation where the money stock is constant for all t.

(a) The optimum strategy for any one type will depend on that of the other. One will therefore have to look for a Nash equilibrium. That is, if $\{w_i\}_t$ is a money wage sequence for type i we must look for a pair $[\{w_1^*\}_t, \{w_2^*\}_t]$ such $[\{w_1\}_t, \{w_2^*\}_t]$ is no better for type 1 for any possible wage sequence different from the starred one and similarly $[\{w_1^*\}_t, \{w_2\}_t]$ is no better for type 2. The existence of such an equilibrium needs technicalities to establish, but let us assume that it can be done. There is no reason to suppose that such a wage sequence leads to a Walrasian equilibrium, since each type has some 'monopoly power'. By that I mean that a small reduction in type 1's money wage does not lead to an unboundedly large increase in the demand for its services.

(b) In general, there are many Nash equilibria. Whatever may be assumed about the uniqueness of a Neoclassical macro-equilibrium, such assumptions are not generally appropriate for Nash equilibria. The multiplicity of Nash equilibria means that the dynamics of the economy cannot, in principle, be predicted from an armchair.

(c) With the constant money stock, if the solution yields money wage reductions then they will be accompanied by changes in real wages. If in the solution type 1 reduces its money wage at $t = 1$, it will then have a lower real wage. Both types will gain employment as firms foresee the higher demand in the next period resulting from higher real cash balances then induced by type 1's lower wage. At $t = 2$ type 1's real wage will still be lower than it would otherwise have been since type 2 had not changed its money wages. On the other hand, type 2's real wage will be higher than it would otherwise have been. It is easy to continue the story. But as long as money wage reductions continue, each type accepts a lower real wage in the relevant period than it would otherwise have had. Each type gains from the money wage reductions of the other. This is so because a money wage reduction of one type will increase both the real wage and the demand for the services of the other type.

(d) These variations in the real wage are the only feasible way in which the types can increase their employment. A constant money wage is not an option if employment is to be increased.

The next step in the argument is now easy to anticipate. Suppose that the money stock is increased as long as both types have involuntary employment. Any proportional policy will do. It is at once obvious that as far as the workers are concerned, they now have a new real option. For instance, for a certain value of the initial relative money wage they can simply sit tight, see employment increase and experience no fall in real wages at all. Notice also that, unlike in the McCallum case, they cannot 'undo' the monetary events to have the same real outcomes as before; for in order that the real stock of money at date 2 be what it was before, money wage reductions would have to be less in date 1 than before, and that would mean a higher real wage at date 1. In general, the change in money policy will have real effects, and, as was the case in lecture I, precisely because it is anticipated.

Now there are many objections that one can raise against this simple model, but I want to argue that some of them suggest that the point that I am making is stronger than it appears.

There are in practice many groups of workers and many firms. There are not constant returns everywhere, and the pricing of goods may also involve game-like considerations. In practice, even if there is adjustment towards a full Walrasian equilibrium, it will be a pretty messy affair. To have rational expectations for such an adjustment path is far more demanding a requirement than to ask for rational expectations about a sequence of equilibria. One thing seems to me quite certain: the uncertainty generated by any such path, the final purpose of which is simply to lead to higher real cash balances, will be very much larger than that generated by constant prices and increasing money stock. If relative prices are 'right', in the sense of being consistent with Walrasian equilibrium, then the changes in relative prices during the process of adjustment to a lower price level are also likely to be a source of mis-information. If a predictable money policy, by reducing the need for price changes, also causes them to change by less or not at all, then on these considerations this will be a real gain to the economy.

Of course, the story that I have just told is not competitive. I do not know how to tell such a story credibly. Here a very small reduction in the money wage of any one unemployed worker should secure him a job. However, the real cash balance effect of such a reduction can be ignored, and so his job will be secured at the expense of others. But there are rational expectations, so that one might think that the only solution is a simultaneous reduction in money wages (by a discrete amount) by all workers. That is, money wage behaviour will obtain exactly the result that could have been achieved at constant money wages by an increase in the stock of money. This, I take it, is McCallum's point. I cannot deny that such a story is logically constructible, but this kind of synchronization of wage behaviour simply seems far-fetched, especially in economies where competitive and unionized labour markets co-exist. Even so, one should notice that the wage reduction mechanism of this story will, on my assumptions, imply a one-period reduction in the real wage which the monetary policy would not. That is because labour inputs precede output by one period. The rational firm at date $t = 0$ will, under competition, leave a price at date $t = 1$ that is independent of demand then, and independent of the money wage at that date.

To this, I now want to add a point that I have made elsewhere (Hahn, 1965). If agents start the story that I have just told with debt denominated in money and the situation is what it is because there has been a large and unpredicted (perhaps unpredictable) shock, then the outlook for price adjustment might be much worse; for during such a process, debtors may go bankrupt. This possibility is a source of a number of technical difficulties, which I leave to one side. What I want to emphasize is that this possibility for any one agent is an added source of uncertainty both for him and for others. Avoiding the need for price level reductions was, as Keynes saw, a way of avoiding such uncertainties. It also may avoid such problems as the destruction of firms with their durable equipment and know-how, which would be perfectly viable in Walrasian equilibrium once it is reached. If someone objects to this because in a rational expectations world debt would be indexed, then, noting the facts of economic history, one can only reply: so much the worse for rational expectations.

So far then I conclude as follows. The Lucasian determination to consider only Walrasian equilibrium prices at each date leaves them with only half a theory. It is as if a physicist considered only objects when at rest on the ground and did not bother himself with a theory of gravity. We should not go to such a physicist to learn about flying. Even so, the Lucasians have the difficulty of multiple Walrasian equilibria which they overcome by ignoring them. I have given an extreme example of this case. However, even in less extreme cases the problem remains, and if there are constant returns, agents have to form quantity expectations. In any case, fully anticipated monetary changes can have real effects as well as no real effects. Once we consider even elementary stories of price adjustment, it is not difficult to find a real role for monetary policy. Price adjustments are costly and a source of uncertainty. The reason why people like McCallum get contrary results is because they have chosen just that *ad hoc* model that delivers the goods. Our simple example of wage adjustment suggests that one is dealing with Nash-like situations and that many adjustment paths will qualify as rational and consistent. I shall be returning to this later.

But now it will be argued that I am pushing against an open door. After all, Lucasians and Monetarists have always allowed for 'short-run' real effects of monetary policy – certainly Friedman has. This is so, but as far as non-random monetary policy is concerned, these real effects are all attributed to the lack of knowledge of the monetary stock (a point that I have already discussed) or to straightforward (albeit rationally made) mistakes. Lucas's Phillips curve work belongs to the latter variety. However, all these real fluctuations are 'bad' and entirely attributable to the monetary authorities. So my first answer is that I have been concerned with real effects in a world where there are no mistakes or lack of information but where agents have to set prices in a decentralized way.

The claim that real effects are 'short-run' is simply without scientific foundation. For one thing, we do not have a remotely convincing model of adjustment. The well-known empirical evidence with its 'variable lags' and reduced forms I have already commented on. Here I confine myself to a single observation. A proper attention to stock and flow relations in an economy, such as arise with durable capital goods and with inventories, will be a potent source of serial correlation. This has already been noted by Lucas (1975). One can leave it to a graduate student to construct simple models where the real effects of a single shock never die out. There is no reason why these shocks should only be monetary ones. The Monetarists always get this wrong because they write down the wrong equations. To a theorist, competitive excess demands depend not only on prices and the stock of money but on stocks of endowments of all kinds. In describing the dynamic motions of the system one needs to have equations describing the movements of all the stocks. The Monetarists, by simply ignoring all stocks other than money, do not have such equations. They should not be surprised then if one does not share their unfounded confidence in the well mannered performance of the economy. The explanation for their almost universal mis-specification is that, being largely macroeconomists, they have no real understanding of Walrasian theory and habitually apply an Arrow–Debreu formulation to a sequence economy.

But while it is surprisingly easy to see the beam in the

Lucasian and Monetarist eye, one must not neglect one's own mote. Indeed, if the truth be told, a large and unruly terrain remains to be traversed before one attains even a tight conceptual grasp of some of the main elements in a satisfactory story. I shall be taking only a few uncertain steps. However, I note that not having the 'true' theory does not logically entail that one cannot recognize a false one.

In my sketch of a possible adjustment story, all sorts of things are open to objection. But here I want to focus on the fact that I departed from perfect competition in telling it. Thus a reduction in money wage yielded only a finite increment in the demand for labour. We do not at present have a theory of an economy in the absence of perfect competition. On the one hand we have some toy models, and on the other propositions that show in what sense a perfectly competitive economy can be shown to be the limit of an imperfectly competitive one. This lack of theory is a serious but much unrecognized problem for macroeconomics. For instance, Keynesian propositions concerning the role of effective demand cannot be given a ready meaning in a perfectly competitive setting. Keynes, whose value theory, such as it was, was entirely Marshallian, left all this in a mess. Recent fixed-price models certainly do not capture what Keynes was after, and in any case are quite unsatisfactory as long as they lack a theory of price formation. But at least they introduced quantity signals into the story which is the beginning of good sense.

When agents are not perfectly competitive, then they must take account of how the economy reacts to their own actions. Their beliefs about this reaction I have called their *conjectures*, and correct beliefs I have called *rational conjectures* (Hahn, 1978). Conjectures must, of course, be distinguished from expectations of events, which do not depend on the actions of the agent. However, I do not now want to go over old ground and highlight the formidable difficulties that remain with the notion of conjectural and rational conjectural equilibria. Instead, I shall take a leaf out of the Lucasian and Monetarist book and go straight to a particular and simple macro-story to make my main point. This concerns the consequences for monetary theory of the abandonment of the perfect competition postulate.

The story is best told in terms of the representative firm and household. I emphasize that I do not regard any such cooking of the books as satisfactory, and therefore regard any conclusions we might reach as provisional.

The representative firm has, for definiteness, a conjectural inverse demand function given by

$$p = ay^\beta \qquad a > 0, \, -1 < \beta < 0.$$

For this I assume it is correct. I propose to treat a as an increasing function of the total output of the economy Y and of cash balances M. Thus

$$a = a(Y, M).$$

I shall save myself a lot of technical discussion if I measure real balances in wage units as Keynes did. This in general will not be consistent with rational conjectures unless there are approximately constant returns to labour. If anyone, therefore, is troubled, let them assume such constant returns. The inclusion of Y is, of course, contrary to Lucasian and Monetarist practice and will be explained shortly. The representative firm treats Y as given, being too small to affect it significantly.

I am interested in the short run and so assume that wage payments are the only variable costs. If there are N firms, we obtain the equilibrium condition[2]

$$y'(\beta + 1)\, a\,(Ny, M)\, y^\beta = w \qquad (1)$$

if each firm takes the money wage w as given. (In the above y' is the marginal product of labour.) For a given w, the above equation has at least one solution y and we give a $(.,.)$ an appropriate form to ensure that it has only one solution, which we can write as $y(w, M)$.

Neglecting the labour market for one moment longer, we note that if $y(w, M)$ is a solution, then at these output levels the good market will be in equilibrium. That follows from rational conjectures. Hence, ignoring the labour equation *à la* Clower, the demand for money will also equal the amount of it available.

Now let us turn to the labour market and assume that, at the given w and the resulting prices, not everyone who wants to can get a job. In order for that to be an equilibrium, there must be no tendency for the wage to change. The wage can be lowered either by the unemployed offering to work for less or by a firm offering less.

I now introduce a twist that Keynes made much of, and which seems to me to have considerable empirical support. The utility of being employed depends not only on the consumption one can then have, but also on one's wage relatively to the prevailing rate. This postulate should certainly not surprise anyone employed in an American university, and in fact should surprise no one given only to mild introspection. It has the following consequence: a worker may be unwilling to accept a particular lower wage for himself at the existing price level but be willing to do so if wages in general are lower. This externality seems to

[2] From arguments that follow, I can only claim that the left-hand side of (1) be no smaller than the right-hand side.

me, as it did to Keynes, to be of considerable practical significance. In particular, it may stop money wage reductions, which are in the interest of workers as a whole.

This calculation depends on the worker's consumption when unemployed ($\bar{w}_u$) and on the probability (λ) of obtaining work at the going wage. I think here of a given proportion of the employed retiring every year while the number capable of work remains constant. I shall assume that the prevailing real wage $\bar{w}$ exceeds $\bar{w}_u$ sufficiently to over-compensate for the disutility of work. (I am here assuming standard hours in each job.) Now write $\bar{U}(\bar{w}_i, \bar{w}_i/\bar{w})$ as the utility when employed at the real wage $\bar{w}_i$ and write $\underline{U}(\bar{w}_u)$ as the utility when unemployed. Then

$$V_u(\bar{w}_u, \bar{w}, \lambda) = (1 - \lambda)\, \underline{U}(\bar{w}_u) + \lambda \bar{U}(\bar{w}, 1)$$

is the expected utility of an unemployed worker. To find his shadow real wage, i.e. the real wage at which he would accept employment when $\bar{w}$ is the prevailing real wage, we solve

$$\bar{U}\left(\bar{w}_i, \frac{\bar{w}_i}{\bar{w}}\right) = V_u(\bar{w}_u, \bar{w}, \lambda).$$

If $\bar{U}$ is continuous and increasing in its argument, it is at once clear that for $\lambda < 1$ the shadow wage will be less than $\bar{w}$. Thus, on its own, the relative wage hypothesis does not prevent the conclusion that workers will be willing to reduce their wage as long as they are involuntarily unemployed.

Something else is needed. The somewhat less attractive of the two, not necessarily alternative, assumptions is that the utility function has a discontinuity at $\bar{w}_i/\bar{w} = 1$. There are various ways in which this could be rationalized. The most appealing is an argument that 'undercutting' on wages is a moral bad. I remind you again that workers are not peanuts. The social norms are of a kind that the offer to work for less than a presently employed group, by however little, is as repugnant as might be the offering of a bribe, however small, to an official. The gain must be discrete to overcome it. Thus, for instance, the utility function may take the form

$$U = \phi(\bar{w}_i) - a \quad \text{for} \quad \frac{\bar{w}_i}{\bar{w}} < 1$$

$$U = \phi(\bar{w}_i) \quad \text{for} \quad \frac{\bar{w}_i}{\bar{w}} \geq 1.$$

I am sure that there is something in this, although I do not know the empirical findings, if any, on this matter. It should, however, be noted that this theory does not imply rigid wages. If unemployment is high, moral repugnance will be overcome.

We are now exactly in the position described by Keynes. Let $\bar{w}_i^*$ solve

$$U(\bar{w}_i, 1) = V_u(\bar{w}_u, \bar{w}, \lambda).$$

Then for $\lambda < 1$ one has $\bar{w}_i^* < \bar{w}$. But this is consistent with

$$U\left(\bar{w}_i^*, \frac{\bar{w}_i^*}{\bar{w}}\right) < V_u(\bar{w}_u, \bar{w}, \lambda).$$

Thus a worker is willing to work at a lower real wage than that prevailing if that lowering is brought about by a rise in the general price level and not if it is brought about by a lowering of his wage relatively to the prevailing one. I now ought to add that this story can also be told in terms of discretely differing skills. If $\bar{w}$ is now the real wage for

i's skill and he can get a job at a lower wage in a lower skill without undercutting there, the desired discontinuity can be attributed to the necessarily discrete utility loss of working below one's skill level.

If $(\bar{w}, \lambda)$ is an equilibrium candidate with $\lambda < 1$, we require

$$\bar{U}\left(\bar{w}', \frac{\bar{w}'}{\bar{w}}\right) < V_u(\bar{w}_u, \bar{w}, \lambda) \quad \text{all} \quad \bar{w}' < \bar{w}$$

$$\bar{U}(\bar{w}, 1) > V_u(\bar{w}_u, \bar{w}, \lambda).$$

The inequality also explains why the representative firm cannot cut wages.

Let me for simplicity use the particular utility function that I have specified. Then for each $\bar{w} > \bar{w}_u$ we can calculate a critical $\lambda(\bar{w})$ such that for $\lambda \geqslant \lambda(\bar{w})$ the unemployed will be unwilling to cut their wage. The formula is

$$\frac{a}{\phi(\bar{w}) - \underline{U}} = 1 - \lambda(\bar{w}) \quad \text{for} \quad \phi(\bar{w}) > \underline{U}.$$

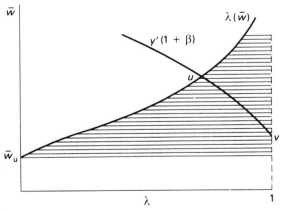

FIGURE 2

This gives $\lambda(\bar{w})$ as an increasing function of $\bar{w}$. The situation is given in figure 2. The shaded area gives the 'no' relative wage cut region. The curve $y'(1+\beta)$ is the marginal revenue product curve. The whole of (uv) are possible equilibria for some stock of real balances. If the prevailing money wage is given, then there is a whole range of the nominal stock that yields 'no wage cut' equilibria. The money stock, therefore, can have potent real effects. But of course it can have no real effects as well: that is, any point on (uv) can remain an equilibrium if the money wage increases in the same proportion as the stock of cash. We have met this situation before. One can tell a Keynesian and a Monetarist expectation story now. Monetarist propaganda has made the beneficent Keynesian story less likely. It is none the less a perfectly logical possibility.

There are considerations that strongly reinforce this account. This is the recognition that the employment of a worker involves the employer in some fixed costs – training costs, administrative costs, production line arrangement costs, etc. There are also costs in hiring a worker below the wage paid to those already in employment. Most implicit contracts seem to make this difficult although available theory has not looked at this problem. In any case, the upshot of all this is that an unemployed worker must make a discrete reduction in his wage to get employed. To reduce your wage by a penny below that prevailing will get you nowhere.

I now consider the utility function as continuous and ask whether a given employment level is consistent with equilibrium; that is, I regard the hiring costs as sunk costs for those who are already in employment. Figure 3 will explain the situation. Assume that the employed consistent with $\bar{\lambda}$ were hired in the past so that their hiring costs were incurred in the past. Then the demand curve for labour has a discontinuity at $(\bar{w}^O, \bar{\lambda})$ since wages have to

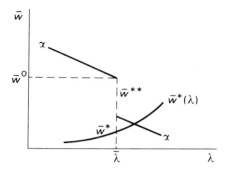

FIGURE 3

fall by a discrete amount to overcome hiring costs. In figure 3 $\bar{w}^{**}$ is the real wage an unemployed labourer is just willing to accept if the prevailing wage is $\bar{w}^O$. On the other hand, $\bar{w}^*$ is the real wage he would accept if all real wages were lower. Figure 3 therefore depicts an equilibrium. Clearly, there will be a stock of money high enough at the given money wage at which real wages are low enough for everyone to increase employment. So the qualitative conclusions of the earlier exercise remain valid for this one.

The small model that I have presented has many gaps, and it does not satisfy standards of completeness or rigour. But in that, it is no worse than most of the macro-models going. Its assumptions seem to me to be a great deal more plausible than those of the Lucasians. I do not have to suppose that the market for labour is the same as that of peanuts, that the unemployed all over the UK are substituting present for future labour, that firms all believe that they can sell what they like at going prices, or that the economy is in continuous Walrasian equilibrium. If I allowed for different skill levels, the story would become even more convincing and could even accommodate a Lucasian fringe labour market. In short, imperfect as it is, what I have shown is that the Lucasians are vastly premature when they urge a scientific claim that fully anticipated monetary changes must be without real effects.

III

Inflation

In this lecture I propose to discuss various aspects of the theory of inflation. It is of course a subject of peculiar topical interest, and I shall not altogether resist the temptation to say something practical. The literature on inflation, with notable exceptions, cannot be read with pleasure or profit. For example, the following incantation runs through so much of recent writings: 'inflation is always and everywhere a monetary phenomenon': I do not know whether this is to be taken empirically or theoretically, or what, whichever way it is taken, it is supposed to mean. Certainly, the price of butter is a butter phenomenon, but this does not seem to be an illuminating observation. If we are kind, then we may interpret it as synonymous with another refrain: 'excessive money growth is a necessary and sufficient condition for inflation'. But this is being kind to be cruel, since we have already studied an example when the claim is false.

But let me start with what is a serious and influential proposition. This is the claim that there is no permanent trade-off between unemployment and inflation. This is often expressed by saying that the long-run Phillips curve is vertical at the natural level of unemployment. More circumspectly and less imprecisely, the proposition might be that the set of rational expectations equilibria is invariant to the inflation rate. Money, so the jargon goes, is not only neutral, but 'superneutral'. The inflation rate, at least in the long run, is thus irrelevant to the real state of the economy and is simply governed by the rate of increase in the monetary stock.

However, in this general form the proposition is generally false, and Monetarists have not, to give them their due, claimed otherwise.

We have already seen in the overlapping generations model that money can be far from superneutral. The inflation rate sets the terms at which present goods can be exchanged for future goods by holding money, and so it will in general affect some of the decisions of households. These are of two kinds: the portfolio decision and the savings decision. On usual assumptions, a higher inflation rate will go with a smaller ratio of financial to real assets in the optimum portfolio. The savings decision derived from an optimum saving plan for infinitely long-lived households will depend on whether the inflation rate has any influence on the real rate of return on marginal savings optimally invested. In addition there is the Tobin effect (1965): if higher inflation rates go with a higher rate of growth in the money stock, then some agents will, depending on how the money is injected, find their disposable spending power increasing faster than would otherwise have been the case. In a simple growth context, this has the effect of raising the steady-state capital–labour ratio so that the extra savings get absorbed. This in turn means that the real rate of return declines with the inflation rate.

To get all this straight in any halfway general context is quite complicated, and as far as I know it has not been done. Much of the literature is concerned with fairly simple growth models and with steady states. Exceptions to this are Brainard and Tobin (1968), who investigate paths of the economy such that at all times the own rates of return of all assets (in terms of *numeraire*) are equalized. But for my present purpose, we need clinch only one simple point. If the real rate of return on non-financial assets in rational expectations equilibrium is invariant to the inflation rate, then in general the real stock of cash cannot be. For simple theory shows that, ignoring possible tangent discontinuities, equilibrium requires the marginal convenience yield of money minus the inflation rate to equal the real rate of return on non-financial assets. Since all other real variables are assumed to have equilibrium values independent of the inflation rate, it must be that higher inflation rates go with a higher marginal convenience and so with a lower real stock of cash. This economizing in real cash balances at higher inflation rates is, rather whimsically, known as the 'shoe-leather' effect. Agents opt for more frequent trips to the bank.

Now there are claims that the 'shoe-leather' effect exhausts the sense in which money is not superneutral. In certain very simple models this is true. For instance, if the economy behaves as if it were carrying out a Ramsey optimum savings programme, its only steady state may occur where the real rate of return is equal to a given constant utility discount rate. Hence, looking only at steady states makes the claim true. In more general settings, it is pretty clear that one will not in general be able to establish rigorously that the 'shoe-leather' effect is the only deviation from superneutrality. On the other hand, real balances are a small fraction of total assets, so that one may perhaps as a first approximation ignore the other real effects which mainly have their source in portfolio substitution – at least in the present class of models.

In any case, this is what has been done by many Monetarists and Lucasians. I know that this must baffle any observer of the contemporary scene. If 'shoe-leather' effects are the only rational expectations effects of inflation, and if it is also argued the economy cannot stay long out of rational expectations equilibrium, it is not immediately clear why the Monetarist politicians are making the unseemly and fanatical fuss about inflation that we observe. Why does Friedman call it the greatest evil? It is true that Professor Minford has calculated consumer surplus triangles for 'shoe-leather' effects, added them up over the infinite future and has concluded that they are large. But I have not been able to persuade myself that these calculations are meant to be taken very seriously. In any event, we have here a problem that I shall have to take up again.

But first I want to return to the vertical Phillips curve – the outward, if perhaps not visible, sign of superneutrality.

The first point to notice is that, taking search costs into account, the Phillips curve is in this theory vertical at a level of unemployment at which the real and shadow wage are the same. That is a level which Keynes and the textbooks for 30 years have called 'full employment'. Looking ahead, we notice that on the short-run Lucasian Phillips curve it is the expected real wage that equals the shadow wage, and the expected real wage differs from the actual real wage that will obtain. It is puzzling to find it put forward as a discovery that a higher inflation rate will not increase the full-employment level of employment: Keynes and Keynesians would not have claimed otherwise. The fact is, of course, that when trade-offs were discussed the unemployment on the horizontal axis was thought of as involuntary. Even so, a trade-off may not exist; this will have to be discussed. But the Lucasians, by denying the possibility of involuntary unemployment – indeed, they profess not to know what it means – have given no reason why anyone should be interested in their trade-off even if it existed.

In fact, the world that they describe quite plainly needs

no macro-policy. Keynesians were concerned with the problem of pushing the economy to its natural rate, not beyond it. If the economy is there already, we can all go home. Even at the micro-level, it is not at all clear that the natural unemployment level should be reduced by policies designed to reduce search. Search may give rise to beneficent externalities, and private decisions may well produce too little search. In any case, the Lucasians have only succeeded in showing that inflation can have no beneficial employment effects by embracing a model in which there are no beneficial employment effects to have.

But let us now look a little more closely at the natural rate itself. It will, I think, be clear that there is no reason to suppose that it is independent of state and date. I shall first consider the unfolding of a rational expectations eqilibrium over states.

It is useful to distinguish between macro-relevant and micro-relevant events. By the former, I mean an event that directly affects the optimum action of many (most) agents. By the latter I mean events that are action-relevant to one agent (or a small group of agents), but not to any other agents. An instance of the former is the occurrence or non-occurrence of the monsoon in India or the decisions of OPEC. An instance of the latter is some exogenous shift in the demand move for a particular product or a firm-specific technical change when the price is small. The occurrence of both types of events may require that the labour allocation in rational expectations equilibrium should change as the events unfold. Macro-relevant events will, in general, also affect the natural employment rate appropriate to them.

The question now is whether this unfolding of the economy can take place at a constant price level. If the answer is yes, then in general this will require a nominal money stock which is state-dependent, for there is no reason to suppose that as the economy unfolds the demand for real balances is invariant. This applies particularly to the succession of macro-relevant events. If the monsoon fails and the money stock is constant, we would expect real cash balances appropriate to that state to be smaller than would be the case for a good monsoon. If the price level is invariant, then the nominal balances will have to depend on the climatic events. Hence a Friedmanesque monetary policy will not in general go with a stable price level (one can easily allow for growth).

If the behaviour of the money stock, on the other hand, is such as to yield a stable price level over states, then it will in general require a fluctuating money wage; for instance, the money wage will have to be lower when the monsoon is bad than when it is good. If money wages are always fixed before the state is known, and if this wage cannot be made conditional on the state, then the policy that keeps the price level constant cannot be consistent with the unfolding of a Walrasian rational expectations equilibrium.

Now, one reason why it may not be possible to make the money wage conditional on the state is that workers cannot observe it. In the monsoon example, this is a little far-fetched. But we can get the same result if we suppose that workers can observe the state but that they cannot calculate its relevance to their own occupation. For the OPEC case, this is not unreasonable. Firms, on the other hand, may be able to observe the state and deduce its implications. This asymmetry between employers' and workers' information gives rise to moral hazard, the implications of which have recently been studied by Grossman and Hart (1981) under the assumption of risk-averse firms. Their investigations are undertaken in the light of the theory of implicit contracts (Azariadis, 1975; Bailey, 1974; Holmström, 1980). They argue that the wage can be conditional on the employment offered because it is easy to see that such an arrangement is credible since the employer loses if he cuts employment in good states. This in turn means that unemployment in bad states will be higher than it would have been in Walrasian spot market equilibrium.

Unfortunately, this is a partial equilibrium result. Indeed, with the exception of Holmström's work, there seems to be no general equilibrium study of economies with contracts. But the moral hazard argument I have just given will require further assumptions in a general equilibrium context. For instance, one could consider a conditioning of the money wage in any one firm on the money wages paid by other firms. Collusion apart, an incentive-compatible Nash equilibrium over macro-states may be achievable in this way. But even for idiosyncratic states, one could argue that the workers know that the firm knows that some of them will leave for some readily available alternative should their firm lower the money wage. This too will reduce moral hazard. One would need to assume that workers are to some extent locked into their firms to maintain the earlier result. This is what Grossman and Hart, and much of contract literature, in fact explicitly or implicitly assume. Clearly, it is not unreasonable to do so, but then the benchmark of the Walrasian spot market equilibrium should also explicitly model this locking in.

In spite of reservations, I think we may accept the proposition that, if bad states are to be accompanied by lower money wages, we would require more unemployment in such states than if the same result were achieved by a higher price level. At least this will be so for bad macro-states. The higher price level itself acts as a signal that times are bad, while a lower money wage is not a trustworthy signal unless unemployment is higher. This result can be precisely established provided there is some locking in. But bad states sooner or later are followed by good states; and if in the latter the appropriate real wage is achieved by a price level that is lower in comparison with bad states, then the economy could unfold without on average generating a rising price level. Even so, I repeat, the nominal money stock will have to depend on the state for this unfolding.

But I now want to argue that this, on average, non-inflationary unfolding has certain difficulties. These arise when the equilibrium requires a different allocation of labour between firms in different states. If there are lock-in effects, then we cannot get a reallocation between states simply by variations of the real wage everywhere over states. A temporary advantage at least must be offered to the worker leaving one job for another to overcome the cost of such a change. Such an advantage may simply arise as a result of being layed off. But in good macro-states such lay-offs may occur only after firms in a relatively advantageous position have been able to expand, which they can only do after they have attracted labour. It certainly seems natural to suppose that relatively fortunate firms raise money wages in order to attract the labour they need. In fact, traditional stories of the price mechanisms would suggest that, if the behaviour of the money stock permits it, the price level will be somewhat lower and the money wage somewhat higher in good states than in the most recent bad state.

What I am now doing is interposing an adjustment story between states. That is, instead of proposing that there exists a function relating, say, the real wages to the state that constitutes a rational expectations equilibrium, I am asking what adjustments in nominal magnitudes can plausibly support it. The argument is at its lowest when different behaviour in nominal magnitudes require different variables to appear in agents' calculations. If money wages are constant, a worker must calculate the probability of lay-off inducing him to make a move elsewhere, while if money wages can change and diverge for a time, he must calculate the probability of a difference in relative wage. Calculating lay-off probabilities involves not identical considerations as calculating the probability of wanting to change one's job because of a relative wage advantage. In any case, I am not claiming more than the textbooks when I argue that variations in relative wages may be the most efficient means of bringing about a reallocation of labour. When this is combined with the earlier argument to explain the obstacles to money wage reductions, we may find that an inflationary unfolding has advantages over a non-inflationary one. That is, money wages are higher in a good state than in the last preceding bad state. If this is the case, then I want to call the resulting inflation the *natural inflation rate*: it is the minimal rate of inflation that is associated with the unfolding of a rational expectations equilibrium.

I cannot claim to have established rigorously that the natural inflation rate is positive. On the other hand, I have given reasons why the nominal process is relevant to the real economy. S. Fisher (1977) has preceded me in this by his discussion of the interaction of contracts and the real economy. To the argument already deduced, we may now add the following one. Workers may find it difficult to observe the current price level. They may base their labour supply decisions on the money wage and a probability distribution over the price level. This will in any case be so if effort is supplied in advance of wage payments. Workers will also regard their price level estimates as independent of the wage paid them in their particular employment. It will then be true that in good states employers can induce a larger labour supply by raising the money wage, when they could not do so by relying on a lower current price level. This would then be another reason why higher money wages should appear in good times.

From all this, I make the following modest inference. It is an unproven assertion that the natural employment rates for different states are independent of nominal mechanisms in general and the inflation rate in particular. As I have noted, equilibrium reasoning of the usual Walrasian kind may be deficient, not only because it does not pay attention to the arrangements that may result from missing Arrow–Debreu markets, or to differences in information, but also because it does not describe an actual allocation mechanism. Thus, for instance, it may be true that, at a certain real wage, there exists an allocation of labour between firms between which labour is indifferent, such that all firms are satisfied. But that does not tell us how this allocation is actually achieved. Paradoxically for a Walrasian, the non-inflationary unfolding would have to rely on quantity signals to bring about the 'correct' labour allocation.

The possibility of a natural inflation rate is, of course, a result of the downward inflexibility of money wages. But this is not an *ex cathedra* postulate, but is derivable from plausible information asymmetries. One should also note that the seemingly strong implication that money wages never fall is due to the fact that I am considering only economies at the natural rate of unemployment. Once our viewpoint is widened, and once we abandon the Lucasian faith that at all times the shadow and market wage coincide, there will also be scope for falling money wages. For then one will have to take account of the competition for jobs between those without contract and those who do have one.

Before proceeding, let me summarize the argument so far. I am not denying that the Phillips curve may be vertical at the natural level of unemployment appropriate to each date and state. With rational expectations, this kind of superneutrality may well hold. What I am arguing is that, when attention is paid to the informational structure of the economy, it may not be possible to attain that kind of equilibrium without inflation. This conclusion relies on the existence of a number of different macro-relevant states. I return to these later in a different context. The basic elements are that workers cannot observe these states directly but firms can, and that wage arrangements have to be made before states are known. The story becomes stronger if workers can observe only the price level of the previous period. I do not assume that government has more information than the public, which is not meaningful here, but only that it has the same information as firms. I know what some of the Lucasian answers will be to all of this. In particular, they will object to the hypothesis that macro-relevant states are not observable to everyone. For instance, this is implausible in the case of monsoons. But it seems to me entirely plausible, for instance, when the relevant events occur abroad. Moreover, it is a matter I think of fact that wage arrangements are made in advance and that these arrangements are not conditional on all possible macro-relevant states. The explanation may just be the cost of doing so. But the consequences are the same.

There is one further matter to be considered. So far, I have been concerned with the variety of natural unemployment rates that arise from the unfolding of states. But there are other considerations, which suggest that it may not be useful to speak of 'the' natural unemployment rate. A sequential rational expectations equilibrium cannot behave better than does an Arrow–Debreu economy. But there is nothing in the latter that allows one to deduce that the equilibrium level of employment is independent of time. This will be true only for special stationary or quasi-stationary cases. I have already noted how much of the recent macro-literature bases itself on this special case. But I have not been able to discover how they justify this habit.

Take the simplest example I can think of: the Solow 1956 growth model. Let us start the story with an initial capital–labour ratio below its steady-state value. We now append to this a Lucasian supply curve of labour derived on a perfect foresight assumption. In particular, workers correctly foresee their rising real wage on the path – it may take a very long time – to steady state. Similarly, the household saving decisions are derived from intertemporal perfect foresight optimization. The model is now different from Solow's, but one can find a path that seeks the steady state and along which the real wage is rising. The natural level of employment will be increasing.

Now suppose the money stock is constant. For what follows, all my arguments would also hold if the money stock is increasing at the rate given by steady-state growth, which will be less than the growth experienced during the adjustment phase. Then, on the usual and especially the Monetarist assumptions, the price level must be falling to provide the extra real cash balances required for higher output. On the simplest Monetarist view, it must be falling at the rate at which output is increasing in excess of its steady-state rate. But that is made up of an increase in the marginal product of labour (as the capital–labour ratio rises) and the increase in work as the real wage rises. Hence the rate of price fall must be greater than the rate of increase in the marginal product of labour, and so money wages will have to be falling all along this path. I have already discussed at length why, when one thinks of the mechanics of wage formation, and in particular notes relative wage deprivation, this path may not in fact be feasible. But I admit that one could tell a story of a very abstract kind where this obstacle would not arise.

But there is now another obvious point. The rate of

price deflation makes money holding more attractive relatively to physical capital. So the actual sequence of natural employment levels is bound to be affected. This is really the Tobin point in a non-steady-state context. But let us make it really dramatic by the following modification: assume that infinitely long-lived capital, once bolted down, cannot be sold. We are starting with a given bolted-down stock and given employment which makes the capital–labour ratio less than its steady-state value. I now want the price and wage level to fall at a rate slightly higher than the marginal product of capital. Of course I want rational expectations. Then there will be a sequence of money stocks such that (a) all savings are in the form of money only, and (b) desired savings (addition to assets) are just equal to the increase in the real money stock. If we abstract from population growth and technical progress the asymptotic state in zero savings, a constant real money stock and a declining nominal stock and price level, it is a rational expectations equilibrium, and everyone fully foresees the money stocks. But the economy never gets to the Solowian steady state. The natural unemployment level certainly here is not invariant to the deflation rate.

But of course, it is not invariant to the inflation rate, either. By monetary policy, fully foreseen, we can speed up the path to the steady state. I have discussed this before and do not now pursue it. I hope to have shown how much 'the' vertical Phillips curve relies on steady-state assumptions. I am pretty sure that this point must have been made in the literature before, and that it is known to many economists. What is puzzling is that we keep hearing so much about there being no trade-off. Is it being supposed that the UK, for instance, is in steady-state equilibrium? Recall also that nowhere in this account have I appealed to an assumption that leads workers not to know their real wage.

Rational expectations economists are, it seems to me, in some difficulty here. One must surely allow governments to be endowed with the facility for rational expectations formation, which is so liberally assigned to the individual agents. Explanations of 'undue' monetary expansion must then turn on elections and seigneurage. But workers can be electorally fooled only if they do not observe the money stock, the behaviour of which is being broadcast daily to the country. Of course, if we allow workers to be temporarily fooled, even if they observe the monetary aggregates, this objection falls away. But then we abandon the rational expectations hypothesis. We can then, however, deduce the behaviour of the money stock from that of the labour market: inflation is generated by the propensity of workers to be fooled and by the advantage to a rational government to fool them. If workers cannot be fooled, then there is no advantage to governments from inflation. That leaves seigneurage. It too depends on a lack of understanding by private agents that the inflation imposes a tax on them. It would be hard to establish that they rationally prefer this form of taxation to more direct methods.

It seems to me, therefore, strongly arguable that the behaviour of the money stock depends on that of the labour market. If there is merit in the arguments for a natural rate of inflation, then this would also explain why the monetary stock behaviour allows inflation. For there are clear advantages to a government to allow the inflation rate that is required by the unfolding of the natural employment level over states and time.

Let us now look at the 'fooling the workers' argument. Lucas deserves much credit for attempting to make this into a piece of coherent theory. Unfortunately, it turned out that this could be done only by supposing that workers do not observe the money stock and this is only very mildly plausible. It seems that we shall have to live with a theory in which workers do not form expectations in a fully rational way: they do not have a true model of the economy. To many people this will be a perfectly acceptable hypothesis.

Now the argument is that, by a monetary injection, we can, by fooling the workers, increase employment above the natural rate at least for a time. Since workers are always on their supply curve, this must mean that they are trading a higher perceived real wage for leisure. But the actual real wage is less than it was since higher employment goes with lower marginal product. So *ex post* there is a clear utility loss to workers. They begin to smell a rat and revise their price expectations upwards. But as long as actual employment exceeds the natural rate the realized utility level is less than it was at the natural rate, although it is always hopefully expected to be higher. Whether such utility disappointments are good for a government's election chances I do not know, but it certainly requires some argument.

However, it is important to understand a central feature of this fooling story: the increase in employment as such is not a desirable outcome for workers. It is the perceived higher real wage that makes it worth their while to supply more labour. So a government cannot take credit for increasing employment: it must take credit for increasing the real wage. In doing so, it will be lying through its teeth and will continually be discovered to be doing so. This is not to me a very plausible scenario.

If labour can be fooled in the way I have described, then it should come as no surprise to anyone that it can also be fooled into believing that a money wage reduction means an equivalent real wage reduction. The Monetarist arguments greatly strengthen my own in support of a natural rate of inflation. For if there are many macro-states – say, owing to fluctuations in the world economy – then a monetary policy designed to have on average no inflation will imply fluctuations in the money wage. But when wages are low, workers will reduce their supply by more than is warranted, and the state may not persist for long enough for them to learn. On the other hand, in the good states they do not observe that their real wage is higher, and employment will increase by less than is warranted if we do not allow money wages to rise. In this world, where the economy may never be at the natural rate appropriate to the state, there is a clear and plausible case for allowing a monetary policy that yields secularly rising prices.

The reason why the Monetarists have missed these rather obvious implications of their 'fooling' theory is that they start with the belief that macro-fluctuations can result only from monetary policy. Not for them OPEC or foreign wars or just sharp changes in the terms of trade. Not for them, in fact, anything but the quasi-stationary state.

There is one further topic to be considered before I pass to the next stage. So far I have entirely neglected unions. One recalls Friedman's famous definition of the natural rate as that rate that would be ground out by a Walrasian system with unions and other imperfections. Neither he nor anyone else has yet done the grinding, and the definition is vacuous and so non-operational. Since unions exist, this is really a very large hole. I am not able to plug it, or indeed to present even a simple rational expectations model with two unions and a competitive sector. The difficulty is that no one knows what unions are out to maximize, or indeed whether they are out to maximize anything. But that is not the only difficulty. When there are unions we are in a game-theoretic situation for two reasons. One arises naturally in the bargaining of union with employer. The other is quite different. In order to form proper expectations, any one union must have a view of what other unions will do. For instance, if all other unions lower their money wage in a bad state, it may not be advantageous for the given union to do so. But in any case, its real wage may go up through the actions of other unions. It is easy to see how, in such a situation, it may be disadvantageous for any one union to bargain first. In short, there is a game between unions. This is plainly pretty complicated, and I believe that it is not at all straightforward to show that some rational expectations equilibrium exists or indeed what the proper equilibrium concept here is. This is a matter of urgent research.

However, I believe that I can argue that the existence of unions strengthens the points that I have already made.

Let us recognize yet a further complication. The union leaders are the agents to the workers' principal. If workers cannot observe relevant states, then it is very plausible that their relative wage position will be an important signal as to the performance of their agent. After all, there is no such thing as a high or low real wage without comparisons. Additionally, movements in the real wage will serve as performance signals. A lowering of the real wage from one period to the next may be due to leader incompetence or to an unobservable state. To this must be added the likelihood that employment itself is regarded as outside the union's control. Many 'optimal' incentive schemes have sharp punishments for falling short of performance criteria (e.g. Mirrlees, 1976). Thus I believe that the presence of unions strongly reinforces everything that I have said concerning the relative wage effect and the reluctance to reduce money wage. If, indeed, there is in that world a natural unemployment rate for each state, then the case for a natural inflation rate is also strengthened.

These considerations are, of course, relevant to the Monetarist doctrine that trade unions do not cause inflation. As usual, they have got hold of the wrong end of the stick. The presence of trade unions raises the inflation rate required to stop the economy having unnecessary unemployment as it fluctuates between states – both macro- and idio-syncratic states. The presence of unions changes the feasible set and causes the optimum policy to have more inflation than would otherwise have been the case. Of course you cannot reach these conclusions if you concentrate on a single steady state, with an error term that cannot be predicted by anyone.

So far I have largely played the Lucasian game of rational expectations and no involuntary unemployment. But now we shall consider more realistic scenarios.

Let me simply stipulate that it is hard to reduce money wages. I have given all sorts of reasons for that. But even if they are not accepted, the matter seems at least as well settled by the facts as is any Monetarist regression. So we start off in a situation where, at the prevailing money wage and prices, more people are willing to work than there are jobs on offer. Eventually money wages may fall but that is beyond our, and in particular the politicians', horizon. In lecture II, I argued that in such a situation increasing the money stock may increase employment. But I also noted that, if agents were all in the grip of the doctrines of Professor Minford, the outcome might simply be an increase in prices and money wages, leaving employment where it was before.

Plainly, something in between is also possible, so that part of the increased money stock goes to increase employment and part to increase money wages and prices. But now we agree that this process may set up an expectation of rising money wages and prices. If we are not to lose our gain in employment, we shall have to accommodate these expectations by continuing to increase the stock of money. But, and this is my central point here, we do not have to live with accelerating inflation; for no one need be fooled, and there is no necessity to keep anyone else fooled. There are of course limits to this process. As involuntary unemployment declines, the *status quo* real wage in wage bargaining increases, and it may therefore be the case that unions will attempt to raise their real wages with predictable consequences. This all depends on how large the involuntary unemployment is to start with and how nicely the unions calculate their power. It also depends on the gap between the real wage and the marginal product. But the main point stands: the policy does not involve moving up along a labour supply curve; hence no fooling and hence no accelerating inflation – just inflation. This then is the price we pay – whatever *that* is judged to be – for a reduction in involuntary unemployment.

But I now want to argue that the case is really much stronger. In this I want to acknowledge the influence of Professor Kaldor.

Throughout these lectures I have meekly accepted the textbook view that the marginal product of labour is never increasing. Of course, if you imagine the world always in perfect competition equilibrium, then it would be true. But in an imperfectly competitive world a rising marginal product is, of course, possible. It is also likely if any expansion in output is accompanied by the installation of newer and technically superior equipment. If this is so, then the real wage can rise and so satisfy the unions. There may still be inflation, but the attempt of unions to increase their real wage as unemployment falls will not, on its own, add to it.

At the end of this story thinking like Monetarists of a stationary state, we are in rational expectations equilibrium. Money wages and prices are expected to rise, and they do rise, at the rate of the increase in the money stock. The number of people out of work is less than it was. The increase in employment, starting from involuntary unemployment, need not be predicated on the mistaken beliefs of workers that their real wages are rising.

In this account of what may be a consequence of a government policy designed to reduce involuntary unemployment, I have allowed for the possibility that it may lead to inflation. I should now like to emphasize that, on Lucasian arguments, it need not do so. I have already made this point in a preliminary way in lecture II. One must suppose that the Lucasians could conceive of a situation in which, momentarily, the money wage is too high relatively to the stock of cash, so that willing workers cannot find work. They will, however, argue that this situation cannot last and money wages will fall. If the economy seeks a rational expectations equilibrium with more employment, it will be one where real wages are lower; that is, there is no real wage resistance. If the money stock is constant, there is also no inflation, and in fact the price level will be lower. Now, using their own fundamental rationality axiom, why should the equivalent equilibrium at the same money wage, higher stock of cash and higher price level not be a perfectly good candidate as well? Even if they argue that the monetary injection was unnecessary since the economy would have got there on its own, how can they maintain that the monetary injection must simply lead to higher prices and wages and nothing else? Only by picking out of a set of rational expectations sequences the single one that is least favourable to public intervention. They have no warrant for that either in theory or in evidence. Indeed, there is no scientific warrant for the cant of 'you cannot spend your way out of a recession' unless you make the hypothesis that there never are recessions such that at the going wages workers in any skill group cannot find a job. The possibility of involuntary unemployment as I have defined it is vital for my argument. Its denial rests on neither theory nor fact.

But because I observe that the world contains unions, that workers have various implicit contracts and that bargaining plays a role that includes moral factors, I am willing to stick by the story that I have sketched. Government intervention may be inflationary, but it will also increase employment and output when there is involuntary unemployment. It is a genuine trade-off between involuntary unemployment and inflation. I think this is the right conclusion. But it is not a theorem. That is because the purely inflationary outcome is one logical possibility. To counteract its possibility, the government may need to engage in anti-Monetarist propaganda.

I have now reached a stage where a topical example will be useful. I suppose that there are not many British economists outside Liverpool and perhaps the London Business School who would not agree that in Britain today there is a huge variety of jobs that the currently unemployed could do and would do at the going wage, but they cannot get hired. I do not deny that there may also be jobs that at the going wage some unemployed would *not* do. Any first-year student will recognize that this is a situation of involuntary unemployment. The fact that there may be jobs the disutility of which is not compensated by the wage is neither here nor there. The extraordinary empirical exercises that take the aggregate supply curve of worker-hours as the Phillips curve need not, I think detain us. In fact, I see no harm for once in accepting as fact what we all know to be true.

What the economy, left to its own devices under some 'non-inflationary' monetary rule, will do in the very long run I know no more than do the Monetarists. I am here interested in the argument that we cannot reduce involuntary unemployment by government policy; in particular, that the old prescribed macro-policies would simply fuel inflation. For my present purposes it is convenient to look

91

at the simplest case, in which the government resorts to the dreaded printing presses to finance extra expenditure. We already know that purely Monetarist answers are a logical possibility. Are there, in fact, in the concrete case I am now considering, also others?

Suppose we consider the Keynesian expectation that the government action will have Keynesian effects with some rise in prices. I have already shown how that might be rational. But I then looked at a closed economy. In actual fact we must consider that the policy would have to go with an expectation of a depreciating exchange rate. So even if the marginal product of labour were non-decreasing, the Keynesian expectations would have to go with a projection of a lower real wage in terms of consumables. An argument in favour of the non-rationality of Keynesian expectations then proceeds by an appeal to real wage resistance on the part of all those already employed. This makes it irrational to expect the policy to have real effects.

If one thinks about this argument, and it may be correct, one is at once arrested by a striking conclusion. If indeed it is correct, then lower money wages with the government passive will not get rid of the problem of involuntary unemployment either. For the situation would be exactly the same, requiring a lower real wage. But then we have argued the market economists into a Keynesian corner: there is no equilibrium with no involuntary unemployment. Their answer that there never is any involuntary unemployment would now be logically untenable.

From this I conclude as follows. If Lucasian and Monetarist theory is correct, so that money wage variability can ensure the absence of involuntary unemployment, then Keynesian expectations under my proposed policy can be rational. If we really cannot use Keynesian policies to help our present ills, then the market will not deliver either. If the market can deliver, then Keynesian policies, although accompanied by increased prices, will do some good.

From this I now conclude that the Monetarist objections to Keynesian policies at the present juncture must rest on a belief in market failure or simply on the unsupported assertion that agents have Monetarist expectations. If the latter, then it might be for the greater social good to tax all Monetarist writings and to subsidize Keynesian ones. If the former, then they had better rethink their models and help in the devising of a workable wage policy.

For what it is worth, and that is not very much, my own impression is that real wage resistance is a serious, if not well understood, problem. It may indeed make Keynesian expectations irrational, but as I have argued, it also makes Keynesian problems more pressing. There then would be no alternative but to intervene in the labour market directly.

Before I leave this topic, I want to make a brief side-remark. Let us suppose for the moment that old-fashioned Keynesian policies work in the usual way. In particular, suppose that the abolition of involuntary unemployment in a no-'fooling' world has entailed a budget deficit. Suppose the economy is now in stationary equilibrium. But how can that be if the stock of financial assets is rising? Only if prices and wages are rising. That of course entails a rise in the monetary value of the deficit. But the inflation rate can be constant with the real deficit and real cash balances constant. So, ultimately, the policy must be inflationary if a permanent budget deficit is needed for the policy.

But once again, my previous conclusions hold. If, in fact, the policy is a device for bringing about real wage reductions which the market on its own would accomplish only slowly, then in the course of our policy the deficit can be successively reduced until it is zero when we get to the equilibrium. This simply follows from the proposition that there is an equilibrium with no involuntary unemployment when no one is fooled. On the other hand, if that is not the case, Keynesian policies will not work better than the market does. In fact, if the market would ultimately have done the job, we can simply set the initial deficit at a level such that the extra tax revenue at a constant tax rate resulting from the reduction in involuntary unemployment will again close it. Of course, once again we require rational Keynesian, and not rational Monetarist, expectations.

I now turn to a different set of questions. Let us suppose the economy is indeed happily settled at a single natural rate and that inflation is proceeding at a steady rate supported and abetted by an appropriate behaviour of the money supply. For some reason, it is desired to reduce or abolish inflation. I have already noted that the logic of some Monetarists makes this child's play: just announce lower money supply figures. But this is not Friedman's view, who believes that the job can be done only through tears and sweat, and no one in Britain today will say that he is not right when you try to do the job his way. Let me consider what is involved here.

We have already discussed the Friedman view: as the money growth is reduced, workers are fooled into believing that the real wage has gone down, while in fact it is going up. So we slide down the supply curve of labour for a bit until they cotton on and we slide up again. For Lucas, the fooling effect is an intertemporal substitution of present for future leisure. Not too much suffering in all of this – certainly tolerable.

I do not consider this view to have any descriptive merit, and I have already given numerous reasons for this. In particular, I have argued that, even in the long run, the government can force the inflation rate below its natural rate only by forcing employment below its natural rate. At this point, however, I am concerned with another aspect, which concerns the stability of the system. It is well known that there are economists who assure us that the fooling of workers cannot last long and that, more or less quickly, they will be sliding up their supply curves again.

I think we can take it that an autonomous change in the money supply rule was not fully foreseen before it was made. Even if it is at once understood and known, it is therefore bound to have real effects. This is quite apart from any fooling of workers. Debt denominated in money and financial assets generally will have unexpected real value and rates of return. Fixed interest debt may, if prices cease rising, have serious cash flow effects on households and firms, including bankruptcies. Anyone who wants to subsume all these under the heading of distribution effects and then ignore them is not a serious economist. However, these impact effects are complex and hard to put into shape for analysis. I think that they are very important, but will none the less not now attempt to disentangle them. For there are even more serious matters to discuss.

Many Monetarists (but not Lucas) never seem to have heard of machines or factories. Certainly, few of them allow the real capital stock to appear in their equations. The charitable way of accounting for this is that they believe that the capital stock at every state and date is exactly what firms and others wanted it to be. This clearly is not an appropriate postulate for our present concerns. One may also remark that it is odd, since Monetarists allow demand to be affected by unforeseen or ill-predicted variations in the real money stock, so that their capital assumption implies that firms can foresee the mistakes of household. It is a rum business. But I need not hammer at this since, as I have said, unforeseen monetary change is here at the centre of our concern.

As the economy moves down the 'short-run' Lucasian

Phillips curve, output will be less than it was expected to be before the natural rate was disturbed by a zealous government. There will be excess capacity. Put differently, the real wage will be higher than it had, rationally, been expected to be when the economy was at the natural rate. Now, excess capacity is bad for investment – both new and replacement. I do not think that this can be controversial: even with rational expectations, it will be so, since there is no virtue in buying capital goods 'early'.

As Lucas has noted (1975) and I have already indicated earlier, once durable capital is brought into the picture, the errors of any date are fossilized in the stock and can in principle haunt the economy for ever. With ingenuity, one can use this to construct a pretty trade cycle model. But anything even halfway satisfactory will also be very difficult. For one thing, there may be many rational expectations paths. There certainly will be many plausible paths if we model the learning of agents. Certainly, the assumption of rational expectations becomes itself strained outside the stationary or quasi-stationary state. In fact, of course involuntary unemployment will develop. Also in fact, no one knows what such a path will look like even qualitatively, and it is surprising that so many claim that they do.

But let me be a little more precise. Suppose that $\bar{w}^*$ is the real wage at the (stationary) steady state and let $P_t = k^t P^*$ with $k > 1$ be the price level at t when the money stock is known to be growing at the rate k. Of course, money wages are growing at the same rate. Real cash balances are constant at $\bar{m}^*$. The capital stock is K^*, and δK^* of this stock is being replaced each period. There are no net savings. Before I proceed, let me stress that everything I have to say will also apply to an economy in steady growth.

Now in a Neoclassical construction, the steady-state capital stock depends on $\bar{w}$, so when looking for the steady-state solution, we solve for $\bar{w}^*$ and $\bar{m}^*$ by setting, say, the excess demand for goods and the excess demand for labour equal to zero when expected values of the unknowns are always equal to the current value. We can write this, ignoring noise terms, as

$$X_i(\bar{w}_t, \bar{m}_t, \bar{w}_{t+1}^e, \bar{m}_{t+1}^e) = 0 \qquad i = \text{goods, labour}$$

$$\bar{w}_{t+1}^e = \bar{w}_{t+1} = \bar{w}_t$$

$$\bar{m}_{t+1}^e = \bar{m}_{t+1} = \bar{m}_t$$

where as usual the superscript e stands for expected. This of course is not strictly correct, since the excess demand at t will depend on the expected path of variables for all firms after t and not just on the expectation for $(t+1)$. But for the moment let me ignore this, since that is indeed what is done in most of the literature.

We now imagine that the economy has been in steady state with inflation up to date T when Mrs Thatcher arrives and sets $k = 1$: the money stock stops growing. In this model superneutrality is obvious to the naked eye – that is, exactly the same stationary-state equilibrium is available after Mrs Thatcher as there was before her. But of course, nominal magnitudes must be lower. But we all know that we would not stay in this stationary state if Mrs Thatcher's arrival had not been properly anticipated. Moreover, workers either do not directly observe the money supply or cannot work out what it implies. They have been correctly anticipating the inflation at the rate k, but they must now learn that prices will somehow be constant in steady state.

To tell the Lucas–Monetarist story, one now needs two real wage rates: the actual and the perceived. The former will influence the demand for labour, the latter the supply. Taking linear expansions of the excess demand functions, and adjoining an expectation formation equation where the revision of expectations depends on the error made, a familiar picture emerges. But it is mis-specified; for, unless the machines and factories can be consumed, the capital stock will be – as long as we are not back in steady state – different from its value appropriate for the prevailing real wage. Put differently, the rate of return – the marginal productivity – of capital will be below its steady-state value. Therefore, in the equations we should have a term for the deviation of the capital stock from its desired value. In the present case, this may simply mean that some of the existing capital is not replaced. But then, if we are to get back to steady state, there is none. It really is not hard, even at this informal level, to see that we are all set to generate a cycle.

But one must here sound a note of caution. If we endow firms with rational expectations, is a cycle really possible? Since there is by assumption asymmetric information between workers and firms, the answer is yes. In particular, the 'error' in the system at any date is not independent of the error of previous dates, since they are reflected in the capital stock. A cyclical story can result. (See Lucas, 1975; for an account for a related more complex model.)

Without constructing a detailed and clearly quite complicated model, this is as far as I can go here. The reason for not actually working an example is simple: I think the theory that I have been discussing to be wrong, and therefore not worthy of detailed examination. I do not think, for the reasons that I have repeatedly spelled out, that Mrs Thatcher's new money rule would lead to a fall in the rate of rise in money wages, certainly not in the first instance, and I would therefore expect involuntary unemployment to develop. Moreover, since I do not think it appropriate to endow firms with rational expectations over an adjustment phase, I feel quite free to suppose that there would be substantial falls in investment. Lastly, because I do not consider perfect competition to be an appropriate assumption, I would not expect price rises to moderate as much as the Monetarists suppose they will. Hence I would expect output and employment to fall by more. Of course, the story does not stop here. Involuntary unemployment may eventually affect money wages, investment and inventory reductions will reduce excesses. But where the economy will go over time, I cannot say. Any model simple enough to yield analytical answers is highly likely to be false.

But that there will be reductions in employment and output, Lucasians and I agree. I believe these effects to be larger than they do. On the other hand, the view that these phenomena are temporary, and that after a suitable delay the economy will be back in steady-state equilibrium, I find no theoretical or indeed empirical evidence to support. At the very least, then, it must be agreed that the policy will have real costs in lost output and misallocations and will be very uncertain in its consequences. All this has to be weighed against Minford's triangles, and I know what the answer should be.

So far, I have considered only the Walrasian natural rate or steady state. In lecture II I discussed the reasons why we should also expect to find non-Walrasian steady states with involuntary unemployment. Since they have all the homogeneity properties of the Walrasian ones, one concludes that if, superneutrality holds for one, then it will do so for the other. Hence the purely monetary inflation that the Monetarists believe in is possible in both states. However, if one is fortunate enough to find oneself in the Walrasian state, then the attempt to cure inflation may drive one to the non-Walrasian state. For there will always be a rational expectations path from one of these equilibria to the other.

In fact, we do not have to invoke any fooling of workers

to get this unpleasant result. The Thatcher axe that I am imagining to fall may induce the expectation of a path of prices such that they cease rising eventually. Associated with this, we can now find a money wage path which leads to higher real wages for the employed and implies involuntary unemployment. This path will also terminate with constant money wage. For I have argued that, at the level of unemployment we reach, money wages will not be reduced by the action of the unemployed. These expectations of prices, money wages and employment are self-fulfilling. The economy finishes up permanently in the low-level equilibrium, and so Minford has to compare the permanent gain in consumers' surplus on money holding from killing inflation with the permanent loss in output and employment. Of course, the usual caveat applies: we do not know which of a number of rational expectations paths an economy will follow after it has received a shock – or, indeed, whether it will follow any rational expectations path. None the less, I should have thought the present possibility to be worrying.

I now want to turn briefly to a situation described in lecture I, where I showed a model in rational expectations equilibrium with a constant stock of money and inflation. However, there was no production. To show a similar result with production, I need increasing returns and imperfect competition on the lines already discussed. At least, I need it if I want to have Lucasian labour market clearing at each date.

Starting in steady state with a given stock of money, let us begin with an expected price path going to infinity but not in finite time. On the usual Monetarist assumptions, this will be associated with a falling sequence of demand and hence output. If there are increasing returns, this will go with a falling marginal product of labour. This in turn, assuming constant demand elasticities, will give us an associated sequence of money wages and so of real wages. However, the falling real wage may induce more or less than the required reduction in the supply of labour. So we may have to amend the price sequence that we started with. However, it can be shown that such an immiserating money wage and price sequence exists (see Appendix). It is a world not of stagflation but of immiserating inflation. This result is no doubt somewhat academic, but not, I think entirely so. The usual assumption that marginal products are everywhere declining is probably empirically very suspect. Perfect competition certainly is so. These bootstrap inflation paths may in fact occur, although one doubts that they are really rational expectations paths over the infinite future.

I am after all this, left with the outstanding problem in inflation theory: Why do people seem to hate it? Why does it drive politicians to destructive frenzy?

I think that the first answer must be quite simply that the Lucasian and Monetarist models are wrong. Consumer surplus triangles could not begin to explain the public reaction that we observe. But that is all we would have in rational expectations perfect competition equilibrium. The fact that Monetarist politicians are most vehement about inflation is a reflection of their inability to understand or think through their own theory. Professor Friedman's vehemence is something else again; it seems to be based on the seigneurage aspect of inflation, which he believes to be an illegitimate form of taxation. The view is maintainable, but it does not explain the public reaction which we observe, either.

Now the obvious way in which the models may be wrong is in their reliance on rational expectations. For instance, the money supply is readily observable, but I doubt that it is much observed. If observed, few people will know what to do with it. To ask them to form expectations in the light of the 'true' model of the economy is to give them a task not to be undertaken by mere humans. So the argument has to be by 'as if'. That argument has deep epistemological flaws. But there is the further drawback that it does not seem to work. The present neurotic preoccupation with inflation cannot come from agents who live in a Sargent–Wallace world. Recall again that no one is supposed to be permanently fooled. Remember also that there are no distribution effects from inflation in a rational expectations world.

To this it could be objected that recent economic history has not been one just of inflation, but of a variability in its rate and in monetary policy which made it impossible to disentangle real states from purely monetary phenomena. After all, rational expectations can require you to use only such information as you have. I think that this Lucasian argument has force, and that with care it could be used to show pretty high utility losses. But it would not be an argument for bringing any inflation rate down – it is an argument for keeping it steady and predictable. Moreover, much of the public complaint seems to be about inflation itself, and not about its variability.

As a matter of fact, of course inflation rates are forecast by all sorts of professional bodies as well as the government. Since they are not made conditional on states, they are quite often wrong. But as a first approximation, agents who believed them would be as rational in their expectations as it is likely to be possible for them to be. Yet they don't like it.

The other objection to my line of argument is that it ignores the tax system. As at present constituted, it of course drives a horse and coaches through superneutrality. It certainly would go a long way towards explaining anti-inflation sentiments in an otherwise Lucasian world. But it does not explain the politicians. They could amend the tax system appropriately. Hostility on their part should be directed against the latter and not against inflation. Moreover, in countries where there is a pretty complete tax indexing, inflation is still regarded as an evil.

There are a number of other factors, like taxation, normally not included in Lucasian models which one might appeal to. For instance, if there is credit rationing, inflation, as Gale (1978) has shown, can have adverse effects on liquidity of companies. If price changing is costly, then Sheshinski and Weiss (1977) have shown that the variance of relative prices is likely to increase with inflation. Numerous other special arguments can be found in the literature. None of them seems to me to be adequate to explain the election of governments whose top priority is the reduction of inflation whatever the consequence. Moreover, none of this explains the conviction of so many people that inflation is bad for employment, output and investment. If these people have the 'true' model of the economy, it cannot be Lucasian.

However, I now note that, if the economy were on one of the bootstrap inflationary paths that I have described earlier – with or without a constant money stock – then inflation and output and employment reductions would go hand in hand. To make one into the cause of the other would not be wrong – things are going badly because of what people expect to happen to prices and wages. I have already agreed that this path was somewhat academic in interest because I insisted on rational expectations and no involuntary unemployment at any time. If those assumptions are replaced with adaptive expectations, and if we permit the labour market not to clear, then it is very easy to construct contractionary inflationary paths. For such a model one could even drop the assumption of increasing returns.

My present tentative view is that this argument is on the

right lines. For the Lucasians, inflation goes with having more than the natural rate of employment, or at least not less, for any length of time. I have argued that inflation can go with long drawn-out contraction and the appearance of involuntary unemployment. Of course, it need not do so. But looking over the past decade, it does not seem a bad description. The behaviour of the money supply along such a bootstrap need, on pure Lucasian arguments, have no effect on the real economy. Trying to reduce inflation in that way would not arrest the decline, at least not with rational expectations: without them, it would make the decline worse.

So in the event, it may not be the rational expectations postulate that is inconsistent with what we observe. Rather, it is the unfounded belief that there is a unique Walrasian rational expectation equilibrium near which any actual economy is always to be found.

It is now of interest to stress one particular matter. If the economy is on a bootstrap inflationary path to a low-level equilibrium with a constant money stock, then, as I have already noted, that rational expectations path cannot be disturbed by properly anticipated money stock changes. A sensible way to arrest it would be by direct intervention in the markets. In fact, this is a situation where incomes policy has a great deal to recommend it. The point I am making here is not the usual one. In the situation that I am describing, fully anticipated monetary policy is not an alternative to incomes policy. It will cure the inflation (subject to the usual caveats), but not the decline. The latter is due to rationally anticipated declines in real balances and real wages.

If we look back over the road that we have travelled, we see that there is a great gap between the Lucasian cup and the discerning lip. This gap, however, is smaller than it is for the Monetarist potion. Lucas's 1972 contribution was of great theoretical interest and of some practical relevance. But it has been succeeded, not least in some of his own writings, by a mindless application of textbook economics. An instance of this is the supply curve of labour hours and the view that that is the Phillips curve. But you don't need three-stage least squares to tell you that, in general, labour is not sold by the hour, that labour hours come in many qualities, and that in many jobs hours cannot be chosen. The proper utility function is likely to be a complex object: having a job probably yields utility rather than disutility. But above all, until there is some theory to tell us how it comes about that we observe only market-clearing wages, there really is no reason to take these exercises seriously. The defence of this way of proceeding is said to be that it yields good economometric fits. I react to this claim somewhat as I do to claims for miraculous cures.

On inflation, this school of thought has been particularly damaging to economic welfare since they have influenced politicians. As I have argued, their famous 'no trade-off' propositions are mendaciously beside the point, since no one ever proposed to get above what used to be called 'full employment' by means of inflation. That there is, as I have argued, even so probably a natural rate of inflation they do not recognize. Above all, they profess the notion of involuntary unemployment to be beyond their comprehension and in some way meaningless. I confess that I sometimes hope that they may come to learn by personal experience what the notion is about. But their most astonishing feat has been to embrace a theory where inflation has negligible costs, and yet to be the most vociferous advocate of curing inflation at any price. I wonder what the electorate would say when it learned that it was all really motivated by a desire to save their loss in consumer surplus on their money holding.

Inflation

What I hope has become clear in this lecture is this: inflation as such is not an outstanding evil, nor do I believe it to be costly in the sense that economists use that term. The reason why inflation matters is to be found in its power to frustrate both desirable market mechanisms and government policy. This was highlighted in my brief discussion of the exchange rate. Real wage resistance frustrates adjustments by any means, market or government. That is why something like incomes policy is almost certainly desirable. But these are considerations that are at present lost in the general belief that inflation is a moral evil in itself. That is a belief for the anthropologist and psychologist to unravel; economists cannot help.

Of course, there is a long way to go before we move from the recognition that these theories are simply wrong to satisfactory constructions. I have tried to give some alternatives, but I confess that they are primitive. The Lucasians have the advantage of a well-worked theory of competitive equilibrium. This theory at the end of the twentieth century can at best be regarded as scaffolding and not as the building. The latter at present has a few bricks, and some of the material that will be needed is lying around. Honest economists will be engaged on the building; they will not claim to have brick and mortar when they are standing on planks. Above all, while there are no objections to tidying up the scaffolding here and there, let the scaffolders be silent on public affairs while the building is nowhere in sight.

Appendix

Rational Expectations Inflation Equilibrium: An Example

In this appendix, I give a simple example of a rational expectations inflation equilibrium with a constant stock of money. As noted in the text, this requires me to assume increasing returns and imperfect competition. The example has all the faults of macroeconomics with representative agents, but one can almost certainly use a device pioneered by Hart (1980) to get round this. To keep things manageable, I assume that all profits are taxed away. This is not at all essential.

The production function is given by

$$y_t = aL_t^\alpha \qquad \text{with } \alpha > 1 \qquad (1)$$

where y is output and L is labour input. There are increasing returns. The firms have a conjectural inverse demand function given by

$$p_t = b_t y_t^\beta \qquad -1 < \beta < 0. \qquad (2)$$

I shall discuss conjectures presently. I assume that β satisfies

$$\alpha(\beta + 1) < 1.$$

Appendix

This, as can be checked, ensures that

$$\frac{d^2}{dL^2}(p \cdot y) < 0$$

so that the firm in a competitive labour market has a well defined maximum.

The representative household maximizes

$$\sum_0^\infty U(c_t, L_t) \, d^t \qquad d < 1$$

subject to

$$c_t + \bar{m}_t = w_t L_t + \frac{p_{t-1}}{p_t} \bar{m}_{t-1}; \ t = 0, 1, 2, \dots \ ; L_t < 1 \quad \text{all } t$$

where $\bar{m}_t$ are real cash balances at t, L_t is labour supplied at t, c_t is consumption at t and w_t is the real wage at t.

I take the special separable utility function

$$U = r \log c - s \log L.$$

Solving, we get the necessary conditions

$$c_{t+1} = \left(\frac{d}{g_t}\right) c_t \tag{3}$$

$$L_{t+1} = \left(\frac{d}{g_t}\right) \left(\frac{w_t}{w_{t+1}}\right) L_t \tag{4}$$

where $g_t = p_{t+1}/p_t$ and p_t is the money price of output at t.

One equilibrium condition is

$$y_t = c_t \qquad \text{all } t.$$

Hence, if the conjectural demand curve is to pass through the actual sale point each t, we need

$$g_t = \left(\frac{b_{t+1}}{b_t}\right) \left(\frac{c_{t+1}}{c_t}\right)^\beta.$$

Using (3), this yields

$$\frac{b_{t+1}}{b_t} = g_t^{(\beta+1)} d^{-\beta}. \tag{5}$$

The evolution of labour requirement for this output sequence is given (from (1)) by

$$\left(\frac{L_{t+1}}{L_t}\right)^* = \left(\frac{c_{t+1}}{c_t}\right)^{1/\alpha} = \left(\frac{d}{g_t}\right)^{1/\alpha} \qquad \text{from (3)} \tag{6}$$

where the asterisk denotes demand by firms.

Now the marginal revenue product must equal the real wage each t, i.e.

$$a(\beta+1)\alpha L_t^{*\alpha-1} = w_t.$$

So

$$\frac{w_t}{w_{t+1}} = \left(\frac{L_t^*}{L_{t+1}^*}\right)^{\alpha-1} \tag{7}$$

Now (4) gives us the evolution of the supply of labour. Substituting (7) into that equation gives

$$L_{t+1} = \left(\frac{d}{g_t}\right) \left(\frac{L_t^*}{L_{t+1}^*}\right)^{\alpha-1} L_t. \tag{8}$$

For equilibrium we need

$$L_t = L_t^* \qquad \text{all } t.$$

Substituting this in (8) gives

$$L_{t+1} = \left(\frac{d}{g_t}\right)^{1/\alpha} L_t \tag{9}$$

so indeed labour demand can be kept equal to labour supply. It is easily checked that profits are always positive given the parameters.

One can now take $g_t = g > 1$ all t and find

$$L_t = \left\{\left(\left(\frac{d}{g}\right)^{1/\alpha}\right)^t\right\} L_0$$

$$w_t = \left\{\left(\left(\frac{d}{g}\right)^{(\alpha-1)/\alpha}\right)^t\right\} w_0$$

So employment goes asymptotically to zero, as does the real wage and real cash balances. Since the goods and labour market are always in equilibrium, so is the market for money.

The example I have chosen can have a steady state only when prices are falling at the rate of time discount. Adding growth alters that if there is no capital.

The example has taken an arbitrary but consistent conjectural demand function. That is, β was chosen arbitrarily. It is not immediately clear how one should calculate the 'true' demand function. Should it be calculated for a constant g or not? Should the labour market be in equilibrium throughout? For my present choice of utility function, different consumptions yield different answers, but on some assumptions one would obtain $\beta = -1$, which would not do. However, I am content to leave the matter here.

Bibliography

Atkinson, A. B. (1969) 'The Timescale of Economic Models: How Long is the Long Run?', *Review of Economic Studies,* 36.

Azariadis, C. (1975) 'Implicit Contracts and Underemployment Equilibria', *Journal of Political Economy,* 83.

Azariadis, C. (1980) 'Self-Fulfilling Prophecies', University of Pennsylvania, mimeo.

Bailey, M. N. (1974) 'Wages and Employment under Uncertain Demand', *Review of Economic Studies,* 41.

Barro, R. (1970) 'Inflation, the Payments Period, and the Demand for Money', *Journal of Political Economy,* 78.

Baumol, W. J. (1952) 'The Transaction Demand for Cash: An Inventory Theoretic Approach', *Quarterly Journal of Economics,* 66.

Bewley, T. (1980) 'The Optimum Quantity of Money', in *Models of Monetary Economics*, ed. J. H. Kareken and N. Wallace. Federal Reserve Bank of Minneapolis.

Brack, W. A. and Scheinkman, J. A. (1980) 'Some Remarks on Monetary Policy in an Overlapping Generations Model', in *Models of Monetary Economics*, ed. J. H. Kareken and N. Wallace. Federal Reserve Bank of Minneapolis.

Brainard, W. C. and Tobin, J. (1968) 'Pitfalls in Financial Model Building', *American Economic Review,* 58.

Cass, D. and Shell, K. (1980) 'In Defence of a Basic Approach', in *Models of Monetary Economies,* ed. J. H. Kareken and N. Wallace. Federal Reserve Bank of Minneapolis.

Cass, D. and Yaari, M. (1967) 'Individual Saving, Aggregate Capital Accumulation and Growth', in *Essays on The Theory of Optimal Growth,* ed. K. Shell. MIT Press.

111

Bibliography

Clower, R. and Howitt, P. (1975) 'The Optimum Timing of Transactions', unpublished.

Deaton, A. and Pesaran, M. H. (1978) 'Testing Non-nested Linear Regression Models', *Econometrica,* 46.

Diamond, P. (1965) 'National Debt in a Neo-classical Growth Model', *American Economic Review,* 55.

Drèze, J. (1974) 'Investment under Private Ownership: Optimality, Equilibrium and Stability', in *Allocation Under Uncertainty: Equilibrium and Optimality,* ed. J. Drèze. Macmillan.

Fisher, S. (1977) 'Long-term Contracts, Rational Expectations and the Optimum Money Supply Rule', *Journal of Political Economy,* 85.

Foley, D. K. and Hellwig, M. (1975) 'Asset Management with Trading Uncertainty', *Review of Economic Studies,* 42.

Friedman, M. (1968) 'The Role of Monetary Policy', *American Economic Review,* 58.

Friedman, M. (1969) *The Optimum Quantity of Money.* Chicago: Aldine.

Gale, D. (1978) 'The Core of a Monetary Economy Without Trust', *Journal of Economic Theory,* 19.

Goldman, S. (1974) 'Flexibility and the Demand for Money', *Journal of Economic Theory,* 9.

Gorman, W. (1953) 'Community Preference Fields', *Econometrica,* 21.

Grandmont, J. M. and Younes, Y. (1972) 'On the Role of Money and the Existence of a Monetary Equilibrium', *Review of Economic Studies,* 39.

Grossman, S. J. and Hart, O. D. (1979) 'A Theory of Competitive Equilibrium in Stock Market Economies', *Econometrica,* 47.

Grossman, S. and Hart, O. D. (1981) 'Implicit Contracts, Moral Hazard and Unemployment', *American Economic Review,* Vol. 71, No. 2.

Hahn, F. H. (1965) 'On Some Problems of Proving the Existence of Equilibrium in a Monetary Economy', in *The Theory of Interest Rates,* ed. F. H. Hahn and F. P. R. Brechling. London: Macmillan.

Hahn, F. H. (1971) 'Equilibrium with Transaction Cost', *Econometrica,* 39.

Hahn, F. H. (1973a) 'On Transaction Costs, Inessential Sequence Economies and Money', *Review of Economic Studies,* 40.

112

Hahn, F. H. (1973b) *On the Notion of Equilibrium in Economics.* Cambridge: University Press.

Hahn, F. H. (1978) 'On Non-Walrasian Equilibria', *Review of Economic Studies,* 45.

Hart, O. D. (1979) 'On Shareholder Unanimity in Large Stock Market Economies', *Econometrica,* 47.

Hart, O. D. (1980) A Model of Imperfect Competition with Keynesian Features, No. 29 S.S.R.C. Project on Risk, Information and Quantity Signals in Economics. Cambridge.

Hicks, J. R. (1934) 'A Suggestion for Simplifying the Theory of Money', *Economica,* 2.

Hicks, J. R. (1939) *Value and Capital.* Oxford: Clarendon Press.

Hicks, J. R. (1967) *Critical Essays in Monetary Theory.* Oxford: Clarendon Press.

Hicks, J. R. (1969) *A Theory of Economic History.* Oxford: University Press.

Holmström, B. (1979) 'Equilibrium Long-Term Labor Contracts', mimeo.

Kareken, J. H. and Wallace, N. (1980) 'Introduction' in *Models of Monetary Economics*, ed. J. H. Kareken and N. Wallace. Federal Reserve Bank of Minneapolis.

Lucas, R. (1972) 'Expectations and the Neutrality of Money', *Journal of Economic Theory,* 4.

Lucas, R. (1975) 'An Equilibrium Model of the Trade Cycle', *Journal of Political Economy,* 83.

Lucas, R. and Rapping, L. (1969) 'Real Wages, Employment and Inflation', *Journal of Political Economy,* 77.

Lundberg, E. (1973) *Studies in the Theory of Economic Expansion.* London: P. S. King.

McCallum, B. T. (1980) 'Hahn's Theoretical Viewpoint on Unemployment: A Comment', *Economica,* 47.

Mirrlees, J. (1969) 'The Dynamic Non-substitution Theorem', *Review of Economic Studies,* 36.

Mirrlees, J. (1976) 'The Optimum Structure of Incentives and Authority within an Organization', *Bell Journal of Economics,* Vol. 7, No. 1.

Myrdal, G. (1939) *Monetary Equilibrium.* London: W. Hodge.

Bibliography

Ostroy, J. M. and Starr, R. M. (1974) 'Money and the Decentralisation of Exchange', *Econometrica, 42*.

Patinkin, D. (1956) *Money, Interest and Prices*. Evanston, Illinois: Row, Peterson and Company.

Radner, R. (1968) 'Competitive Equilibrium under Uncertainty', *Econometrica, 36*.

Samuelson, P. A. (1958) 'An Exact Consumption-Loan Model of Interest with *or* without the Social Contrivance of Money', *Journal of Political Economy, 66*.

Scheinkman, J. A. (1980) 'Discussion of N. Wallace, "The Overlapping Generations Model of Fiat Money"', in *Models of Monetary Economics*, ed. J. H. Kareken and N. Wallace. Federal Reserve Bank of Minneapolis.

Sheshinski, E. and Weiss, Y. (1977) 'Inflation and Costs of Price Adjustment', *Review of Economic Studies*, 44.

Starrett, D. (1973) 'Inefficiency and the Demand for Money in a Sequence Economy', *Review of Economic Studies, 40*.

Tobin, J. (1956) 'The Interest Elasticity of Transactions Demand for Cash', *Review of Economics and Statistics, 25*.

Tobin, J. (1965) 'Money and Economic Growth', *Econometrica, 33*.

Tobin, J. (1980) 'Discussion of Overlapping Generations Models', in *Models of Monetary Economics, ed. J. H. Kareken and N. Wallace. Federal Reserve Bank of Minneapolis.

Wallace, N. (1980) 'The Overlapping Generations Model of Fiat Money', in *Models of Monetary Economics, ed. J. H. Kareken and N. Wallace. Federal Reserve Bank of Minneapolis.

Wallace, N. (1981) Submission for NSF grant.

Index